NEW EDITION

UNDERSTANDING WILLS AND ESTATE PLANNING

IMPORTANT THINGS TO CONSIDER WHEN PLANNING FOR THE FUTURE

Rod Cunich

Published by:
Wilkinson Publishing Pty Ltd
ACN 006 042 173
Level 4, 2 Collins Street
Melbourne, Vic 3000
Ph: 03 9654 5446
www.wilkinsonpublishing.com.au

A catalogue record for this book is available from the National Library of Australia

Planned date of publication: 01-2019
Title: Understanding Wills and Estate Planning
ISBN(s): 9781925642681: Printed - Paperback

Design by Spike Creative Pty Ltd
Ph: (03) 9427 9500
spikecreative.com.au

Printed and bound in Australia by Griffin Press, part of Ovato.

About the Author

Rod Cunich is a lawyer with four decades of experience assisting individuals and businesses with a broad range of legal and commercial issues. With a background in company, trust and insolvency law, Rod is especially interested in helping people with personal estate planning and business succession planning, where clear communication, practical skills and life experience are as critical as legal knowledge.

Rod holds a Masters of Law (Estate Planning) and is a registered 'Trust and Estates Professional' (TEP) whose qualification is internationally recognised.

Rod regularly speaks at national and international conferences for law professionals and members of the public interested in legal topics. One of his great skills is simplifying complex issues by using language that everyone can understand.

Rod is based in Sydney but practices nationwide. You are invited to visit his website to find out more about his mentoring, education, estate planning and asset protection services: www.rodcunichlawyer.com/.

Introduction

Everybody needs a Will. That's why this book is written for 'everybody'.

The purpose of this book is to explain in simple terms the processes and procedures needed to prepare an effective Will and other estate planning documents. Where relevant, I've listed options at various stages to help with your decision-making.

Most of us expect to live to a ripe old age but the reality is, we could pass away at any time. So, it's important to start planning before it's too late.

Lots of 'just-in-case' decisions need to be made now. For example, there could be a time in the future when you're still alive but can't make decisions for yourself. That day could be tomorrow.

Estate planning isn't all about death. It includes things like 'guardianship' and 'Power of Attorney' which most people don't even think about. These involve appointing someone to make medical, financial or legal decisions on your behalf, if you can't, either because of failing mental capacity, or because you're in a coma after someone ran a red light. If you nominate your 'sister Sue' to make decisions for you, so be it. Otherwise it's up to the courts, and they may pick your 'big brother Bill', the weightlifter you never liked, and is the family 'black sheep'.

That's quite true of almost every area of this book — either make the decision yourself or it's out of your hands. Good intentions aside, there is no guarantee that your unwritten wishes will be carried out. (It can be tough enough getting the written ones through!)

Then there are issues like 'tax minimisation', 'asset protection', 'superannuation planning' and 'business exit planning'. Again, issues often neglected because there is 'always tomorrow' to get around to it. None of these matters are pressing until a crisis occurs or time simply slips by unnoticed. My father-in-law once said, 'why do today what you can put off till tomorrow', and it seems many of us agree. In many cases no one can make these decisions for us as they take time to implement and if not addressed by us when we can, we end up having to live with the consequences.

Rod Cunich TEP
Estate Planning and Wealth Protection

Contents

I. Write a Will

Write a Will.

It's no big deal.

Close to 45% of Australian adults don't have one. Many of those who do are unaware that their existing Wills are inappropriate for their current circumstances and need updating.

If you have no Will, the distribution of your estate will be unnecessarily delayed. Extra costs will be incurred because an application will have to be made to the courts to appoint an administrator to your estate. You won't get to choose who manages your estate, nor will you get to select who receives your property.

With no Will, your estate will be distributed in accordance with a statutory formula. Your own wishes won't be taken into consideration because – remember – you left none. Under succession laws, former spouses, de factos, and in some cases even short-term partners may end up with a portion of your estate. It's all a bit 'up in the air'. That's why everybody should write a Will.

People say to me, 'Rod, I'm only 30 or 40, why should I bother with all this stuff now?' or 'I don't own much so why bother?'

As for the timing I invariably reply, 'because by the time you get around to doing it, it may be too late! In fact, you may procrastinate for so long that you never write one at all'. And on the issue of wealth, 'it's not only about wealth, a Will covers off on other immediate issues you should address such as guardianship of children and your digital assets. Besides, if you do it now it's in place when you do accumulate enough assets to lose sleep over'.

Many young people don't bother to write a Will because they associate dying with old age. They think (if they think about it at all) that writing a Will is something someone does when approaching death, which is supposedly when you're older. A glance at the daily news reminds us that death doesn't respect age. Even guardianship, which is generally associated with aged care, can be an issue for young people, under certain circumstances.

Just as signing a Power of Attorney doesn't make you mentally incompetent, signing a Will won't kill you. At worst it's a paper cut, I promise you.

I recommend you make the decision to act now so you can do so without pressure and maximise the chances of making the right decision.

And look what happens when you don't write one!

| ACTION | Writing your Will is your first step. |

CASE STUDY

WHAT CAN HAPPEN WITHOUT A WILL

Mary was an abused child. Because of this, she left home as soon as she could, at age 16. She never spoke to her parents again. With that part of her life behind her, Mary put herself through university and started a career.

Then she met Joe, a successful stockbroker who she married. Joe was slightly older than Mary. They enjoyed a good marriage, and Joe's family became her family. Alas, after eight years of marriage, Mary and Joe died in a car accident. They had no kids. Neither of them had a Will.

Being the older of the two, Joe was deemed to have died first and his wealth notionally passed to Mary. Under the intestacy laws all of Mary's acquired wealth then passed to her estranged parents – the last people on earth to whom she would have wished to leave her estate. To rub salt into the wound – Joe's family got nothing.

INTESTACY LAWS

Each state and territory in Australia has intestacy laws that operate as a de facto Will for those who leave no Will when they die.

Where there is no Will, assets typically go to the spouse. In some states a spouse must share the assets with children (so there isn't even a consistent outcome across the country). If the spouse is predeceased, assets usually go to the children equally. If there are no children, typically they will go to the parents, and from the parents down to other family members.

If there is a spouse (even if separated) and a de facto, then things get interesting because in some states they must divide the estate 'by agreement'. Throw children into the mix and you have the plot for a horror movie!

This procedure requires an application to the court, which is more expensive than a probate application because someone has to start from scratch. Legal costs escalate, delays often occur and claims against the estate often come out of the woodwork by people who assert they should have received a benefit that wasn't provided for in the statutory formula.

Am I scaremongering or being a tad melodramatic? If only it were fantasy. Ever heard the saying that 'truth is stranger than fiction'? Search around the internet for stories and court decisions about family hardship and disputes arising from the absence of a Will or a 'proper' Will. The reality is that living without a Will is like playing Russian Roulette with your assets.

WHAT IS A WILL?

A written Will determines how your assets are to be divided on death. It's a formal document that enables you to pass assets from one generation to the next. A Will must comply with strict legal requirements concerning both the form of the document and the way it's executed.

The courts will sometimes accept a document that doesn't satisfy all the technical requirements, provided they're satisfied that it's genuine and that it truly represents the wishes of the person involved. It can be difficult to prove. It's much easier to write a proper Will than to have your grieving family spending time and money satisfying the courts that a document or video is truly a Will.

Formal requirements. Most lay people aren't aware of the formal legal requirements of completing a Will, so they can very easily overlook them. Let me tell you a bit more about them to give you a better understanding.

The necessary formalities of a legal Will are:

1.   Signature,
2.   **Date**,
3.   A clear statement that it's the **final Will**, i.e. an opening phrase such as: 'This is my last Will and Testament...' (In the absence of that, it might be nothing more than a jotting of what you might be contemplating at the time.)
4.   **Two witnesses** who aren't benefactors. A lawyer need not be present.
5.   **The willmaker and both witnesses** must all observe each other sign the document.

Some people literally pull out a sheet of paper, write 'When I die I want my assets to go X', they get two witnesses to sign and date it – and that's their Will. Or so they hope.

All too often they get it wrong. Succession law and asset ownership issues can appear deceivingly simple, when the reality is they aren't.

OPTIONS

Some people use a cheap do-it-yourself Will kit (DIY). Something bought from their local Post Office shop or newsagency. Others use an equally inexpensive online template. Most do not intelligently assess your needs and address them. Rather, you must guess or assume the document will satisfactorily address all your issues.

Many people believe they're saving money choosing the cheapest options and that there's no real need to pay a lawyer to prepare a Will. After all, aren't they very simple documents that anyone can prepare? You can be forgiven for thinking so, but you would be wrong.

You'll discover during reading this book that a professionally prepared Will, where the complexities of the law and your individual assets are considered, doesn't cost much. In fact, relatively little when the cost of making an error is factored in.

A lot of people use a template Will. They fill it in themselves and hope for the best. Those types of Wills are sometimes enough. It's true that they do address many general needs. But whether they do or don't satisfy an individual's needs is very much a roll of the dice. Because if it does, it means their affairs are extremely simple and they don't need any bells or whistles. The problem with do-it-yourself Wills are the complications in their affairs that require special attention that they aren't aware of.

The danger of doing it yourself is you don't know whether the simple Will covers everything, or whether you need something more. The point is: **_lay people don't know what they don't know._**

Recommendation: Have your personal requirements assessed before you jump in the deep end. See a lawyer or visit my website and do your own introductory estate planning self-assessment using my 'Estate Planning Self-Assessment Tool': www.rodcunichlawyer.com/forms/
Or fill in the short version of this tool set out in Schedule 2 of this book.

It's a great starting point to help you identify your personal requirements. You will at least know what issues must be addressed, even if you don't have all the answers.

COMPLICATIONS

Individuals may have complications within their personal or financial affairs that require special advice and special treatment. Complications they often don't realise exist, or if they do, they might not know the options available to deal with them.

Examples of common complications requiring special attention:
- having a beneficiary who is a spendthrift, married to a gambler, facing divorce or exposed to financial risk – any of which could result in an inheritance being lost
- there is a blended family where there are completing interests in assets on death
- there is a family trust whose assets aren't controlled by a Will
- there is a self-managed superannuation fund and there is an unknown need for a superannuation 'Binding Death Benefit Nomination'
- they are separated from a partner/spouse and not yet had a property settlement
- there are step-children or other non-relatives who are (or claim to be) dependents and could challenge the Will
- not understanding potential taxation implications of: children living overseas, the relationship with the person who receives superannuation death benefits, the impact of death on pre-CGT assets and multiple other taxation issues that arise on death
- 'A' owns property jointly with 'B'. B will automatically inherit total ownership on A's interest on death, BUT A wants to leave their interest to 'C'
- a gift of shares or other property that they or their attorney sell before they die, complications associated with adjusting for loans made to children, trusts or others, and borrowings
- a whole range of things that people overlook because they don't know that these things are relevant.

Some of those issues will be easy to address. Others will be more complex.

Relationship breakdowns invariably complicate people's lives. And these issues can certainly affect a Will. Even though children of a prior relationship may have been paid money (through a family court settlement) these children may still have a right to claim against the estate and challenge the Will in competition with a new family. People often overlook that possibility.

COST

Compared to other legal procedures, the cost of having a Will prepared is relatively inexpensive.

A standard Will prepared by a lawyer can cost as little as $400 or $500, sometimes less.

Wouldn't you invest that sort of money for the peace of mind it can provide knowing it's been done properly?

There are of course more expensive estate planning packages available for those who have complex personal or financial affairs, but they form a small part of our community.

But why pay I hear you ask?

You might ask 'Why pay when I can do an unassisted DIY Will, get it done for free or maybe pay just a nominal sum? After all, some Will-Kits cost as little as $4.50'.

Let me share a word of caution. The value and true worth of a properly prepared Will has been undermined and people have been misled into believing that they're 'such simple documents' that anyone can prepare a Will. 'They are so cheap, it must be a simple exercise' I've often heard it said. The formal legal requirements, the high chance of making an error or overlooking something and the dire consequences of getting it wrong have evaporated in the minds of many. Like a sharp knife in the hands of a child, all may be OK but there is plenty of scope for disaster.

Who is responsible for creating this misconception? We lawyers and Trustee Companies must shoulder most of the blame because many have drafted Wills for clients for next to nothing.

Historically lawyers often have a long-term relationship with their clients (i.e. the family lawyer) and preparing Wills has been treated as bit of a 'freebie' or as a loss-lead to maintain the relationship knowing that in the long term the investment of their time will pay dividends. Dividends? Think about it, someday you'll die, and if the lawyer is storing your original Will, they'll make the money from applying to the court for probate and administering your estate. Some might see this as good business sense and a good service offering to clients, but it does have the side effect of leading people to believe that Wills are easy and simple because lawyers barely charge anything for them.

That attitude is out there now, and it's common. It's hard to convince many people otherwise. When confronted by people with this mindset I'm made to feel like I'm offering unwanted fries with their burger when I offer estate planning advice. I (and many estate planning lawyers) are happy to provide initial no obligation help but I discourage anyone (including lawyers) from doing 'cheap wills' because it all too often results in corners being cut (time is money after all) and inadequate attention being given to the detail.

There are two consequences of these practices:
- Lawyers lose money preparing Wills.
- By undercharging, lawyers have contributed to the devaluing of the importance and complexity of Wills in the minds of the public.

The result? The public is given the impression that, 'Wills are so simple lawyers even give them away, so I should be able to do one myself or at the very least buy a cheap one anywhere'. That's a general mindset that lawyers are partly responsible for creating. It's wrong and dangerous.

The other group responsible for creating this impression are the trustee companies, including **state government-controlled trustee companies**. Many run campaigns saying 'we will do your Will for free' – which is particularly appealing to elderly people who might be watching their pennies.

These trustees will suggest something like this,
'If you're concerned that:
- there may be some argy-bargy amongst your kids, or
- you don't wish to burden them with the job,
then appoint us as your executor or your backup executor.'

Older people might consider this and say, 'Fine, I'll appoint you as executor, you understand this sort of thing'.

What people often don't appreciate is that most trustee companies give away Wills to strangers because they're going to make a lot of money out of the probate and estate administration – much more than most lawyers would who offer many of the same services. They aren't doing anyone a favour.

Trustee companies quite often charge the sort of fees lawyers charge for doing those jobs, but **they also charge a commission** on top of that, based on the gross value of the estate. That could be anything from 1%-5% – so it's important to read the fine print and not fall into that trap. At this time there is only one government backed trustee company that I'm aware of that doesn't charge a commission as a matter of course. Some lawyers do the same thing so be cautious.

Another consequence of lawyers and trustee companies undertaking cheap or free Wills as a loss-lead is this: how much time would you think that a lawyer will spend understanding their client's needs and addressing them meaningfully? As time is money, lawyers and trustee companies have been known to take as little time as possible.

Because they're losing money on the transaction, there is a risk that lawyers and trustee companies will get the client in, get the basic instructions, write a basic Will, and then get them out. Time is money. Whether the Will is appropriate may be another thing all together.

I once knew a solicitor who said, 'I've being doing Wills for decades and never once had the need to prepare anything other than a simple standard Will'. He subsequently attended a lecture I delivered to lawyers about Wills and the issues that need to be considered. Two weeks later this same lawyer said to me 'It's amazing, since your lecture I've had three families see me who needed more than a standard simple will'. I wonder how many he overlooked in the previous decades?

Without proper advice, you may well end up with a standard Will that doesn't consider your individual family and financial circumstances. This could be quite dangerous for the future of your estate. Don't get me wrong, many standard Wills are perfectly fine. The ones that cause problems are those where complications are overlooked because of lack of thorough investigation and this takes time and costs money.

There are simply no free lunches and you get what you pay for. Nothing more, but sometimes, a lot less.

Simple needs or more complex – which category do you fall into?

Answer: You probably need to be an experienced succession lawyer to make that call.

SAFE KEEPING

The decision where to store a Will, once signed, rests with you, the individual client. It's up to you to determine what you want to do with it. Some clients want to take it home; others want to deposit it with the bank.

Most lawyers and trustee companies will offer to store the Will and other documents (like title deeds) in safe custody at no cost.

Is there anything wrong with this practice?

No, it provides the client certainty and security for their documents but more than that, it increases the chances that their executor will engage the client's preferred lawyer to look after their family's interests during the probate and estate administration process. It makes good sense for all concerned. It also assists the family expedite the probate application when that time comes.

How often do you need to redo/check your Will?

The next question is: 'how often should I review my Will?'

Answer: You should review it every time there's a major change in your financial or family life.

It could be an acquisition or a disposal of an asset or business. It could be a birth, a death or a marriage of someone affected by your Will. When a big event like that happens, you should revisit the Will, think about it and ask, 'have I already covered that event as a contingency in the Will? If not – should I perhaps amend it?' If you can't work that out, ask a lawyer.

In nine out of ten cases the answer will be 'no you don't have to amend the Will because it already takes into account that situation'. But occasionally, a paragraph may need re-working to bring it up-to-date.

If it's a marriage breakdown then you probably only require a small (but very important) tweak. If a major benefactor has died, you may need more. Computer technology has made this all pretty simple. You just ask your lawyer to change the existing digital copy of the Will on the file, reprint and re-execute it. You are only charged for the amendment.

There are some circumstances though where you'll need to completely redo your Will.

1st Will:	A person might write their first Will in their 20s or 30s with a partner, no children and a property with a mortgage.
2nd Will:	By 40 they've got children, small investments, a mortgage and other debts.
3rd Will:	By 50 one of their children might be in a failing marriage, another in a high-risk business, and the third with a disability – who struggles to handle money. Their future inheritance is at risk and a simple Will won't help them protect their inheritance.
4th Will:	By 65 they find they've made a reasonable amount of money over time, with a paid-up mortgage, family trust, investment property and perhaps superannuation and life policies. The risks previously identified become even bigger in magnitude. Managing the estate will be much more complex as many of the assets may bypass the estate and require separate management (such as superannuation death benefits, insurance proceeds, trust assets and interest in jointly owned assets).

Managing all the issues that flow from those things requires a bespoke (individually crafted) Will and estate planning, designed to address those specific circumstances.

Again, that Will should be reviewed whenever there's a major change.

ACTION As a catch-all, even in the absence of a major event, I recommend that people should review their Will once every three years.

I didn't say re-write or revamp. I simply suggest pulling it out every three years, re-reading it, thinking about it and simply checking that it all still makes sense in your current circumstances.

Unless you live a turbulent life, most times you'll say, 'that's still okay...' and slip it back into your sock drawer. If not, ask your lawyer.

FACTORS TO CONSIDER

An estate is usually composed of physical belongings (such as cash, clothes, jewellery, cars and the family home) as well as investments such as superannuation or share portfolio and even digital assets such as photos and documents stored on a computer or in the cloud (many lawyers are still getting their heads around that concept).

The **protection of inheritances** is one important factor to consider. If a beneficiary faces:
*   a failed marriage (over 1/3 of marriages fail),
*   remarriage,
*   bankruptcy,
*   loss of mental capacity,
*   drug or gambling dependency,
*   spending problems,
*   gambling or spendthrift spouse, or
*   family disputes

What happens to their inheritance when they receive it?

Does part, or even all your hard-earned wealth end up in the hands of a child's ex-spouse, their creditors or their drug dealer? (Maybe one of our local casinos will end up the ultimate beneficiary!)

A second consideration is the **minimisation of the tax** burden for your estate and your beneficiaries, once they take ownership of your property.

A third, important consideration is deciding upon **guardians** to care for your children if they're still minors when you pass away. Assuming it will be their god-parents or step-parent would be wrong. You need to formally nominate someone, and you can do so in your will.

Preparing a Will is part of the bigger picture of estate planning (sometimes referred to as succession planning – the terms are often interchangeable). BUT IS IT ALL ABOUT DEATH?

Definitely not. Estate planning is also about the here and now, as much as it's about what happens when you pass away. To protect your family and your property you should consider problems that you, or they, may face during your lifetime – not just when you pass away. You can be as much trouble while alive as you can be on death.

Failing health, failing mental capacity, accidents, financial management, insurance needs, debt management, business succession, investment planning, wealth accumulation for retirement and aged care are just a few of the issues that a comprehensive estate plan can and should address.

The legal components of estate planning should only be part of your broader estate planning strategy. A well-thought-out plan should include legal documents that are coordinated with your retirement, investment and wealth accumulation strategies. It often requires a coordinated and cooperative approach to a client's planning by their lawyer, accountant, insurance adviser and investment advisor. Professionals operating independently of each other can (and often does) result in chaos. Legal, financial and personal affairs resembling a bowl of tangled spaghetti isn't the ideal structured pathway to the future.

A structured strategy and proper documentation will ensure that all parties are on the same page at each stage of your life journey – from now to death and beyond. A good plan is capable of being followed as the years roll on. An estate planning lawyer can work in tandem with your accountant, financial planner and insurance adviser. Doing this provides security and certainty for you and your family. Spending time and money now on the right professional advice will save you and your family heartache in the future.

THE MOTHER, HER SON AND HER LOVER

Dan is an only child. He had worked for 23 years in the family business. First it was owned and controlled by Dan's father, but after his death, ownership of it passed to Dan's 70-year-old mother Pat, who had accumulated a large estate. Dan stood in line to inherit the business and all of Pat's wealth.

Then Pat became re-acquainted with Frank, an old family friend. They were both looking for companionship in their later years. After a time, Frank moved into Pat's house and they lived together as a couple. Three years later Pat passed away without a Will. And in the absence of a Will, the Intestacy Laws govern who benefits from her estate.

Under these laws in NSW (it varies from state to state), being Pat's de facto, Frank inherited the first $350,000 of the estate (a legacy sum fixed by legislation, and CPI adjusted), plus all Pat's personal effects and 50% of the balance of the estate. Dan got 50% of the balance, *which wasn't enough for Dan to guarantee the continued survival of the business. Dan now faces an uncertain future. Thankfully he didn't live in Western Australia where he'd have been even worse off. It's a lucky dip.*

LESSON

In the absence of a Will, the courts determine the distribution of an estate according to the intestacy laws of the state or territory. These laws may not match your wishes.

EXECUTOR

Choosing the right executor is as important as choosing your Guardian and Power of Attorney. An executor's job isn't for the faint hearted. Ask anyone who has taken on that role; they'll tell you that the duties can be difficult, stressful and time consuming. These responsibilities include applying for probate and administering and distributing your estate. In some cases (too many) it also involves fending off attacks on the estate by wannabe beneficiaries.

When weighing up your potential executor, make sure you choose a capable, trustworthy person. You don't need a professional person to act as executor (for example, a lawyer) but sometimes it's a great advantage. Any person with mental capacity and over the age of 18 years can be appointed. This includes your children and beneficiaries. Yes, your children can be appointed as executors, but are unable to act until they're 18 years of age.

Whoever is appointed will have to be on hand when his or her services are required. As a rule of thumb, I suggest you avoid appointing elderly people or those who live far away.

Whom you choose will depend on:
- **Complexity.** The complexity of your financial and family affairs.
- **Skills.** The skills of the potential candidates.
- **Negotiating skills.** The likelihood the executor will have to deal with disputes over the estate.
- **Impartiality.** Whether or not the executor will have a conflict of interest. If they manage the estate and are also beneficiary, others in the family may perceive favouritism. If they don't get on in any way, sharing the role of executor can almost guarantee disputes.

The most common choices are:
- Wife, husband, partner or children.
- Friend or business partner.
- Professional adviser – possibly a lawyer, accountant or both.
- A trustee company.

It's preferable to have more than one executor and/or **a backup executor** in case one executor dies, is unable to act, or starts to act but can't continue to do so. Alternatively, you can nominate a firm of lawyers or a trustee company, but it's important that you enquire about their fees and charges beforehand.

The executor is required to gather all the assets, secure them, pay existing debts and then distribute assets in accordance with the terms of the Will.

Estate administration refers to the process that the executor of an estate goes through to manage and distribute the estate assets in accordance with the terms of the Will.

| Understanding Wills and Estate Planning

2. Start planning now

Estate Planning is like planning a trip to visit a friend who has moved to a new house.

Sometimes it's simple and other times it's more complex, depending on where they have moved:

- Around the corner − minimum planning needed.
- To a distant suburb you're not familiar with − before setting off check the address, how to get there and how long it will take.
- To a new city you're not familiar with − same as a distant suburb but the travel logistics will require a lot more planning.
- To a new country − same as a new city but with added planning, attention to timing, cost of travel, transport to and from airports and the time away from home.

The complexity of each plan varies, but the time to do the planning in each case is before you leave home. It's too late to think about getting a passport when you arrive at the airport.

In other words, the time to plan is now. Your journey through life has already begun and if you haven't got your plan already in place, you need to do so before you meet any unexpected barrier to your progress.

Another reason to plan ahead: 'if you haven't identified where you are going and how to get there, you never will'.

BEGINNING THE PLANNING DISCUSSION

Most people feel somewhat uncomfortable discussing their own mortality with members of their family. Death is a taboo topic for many, but it's not just death and the division of property after someone dies that is neglected. Unless discussed and planned for, there is no certainty about what happens if, through accident or the ageing process, a person loses the ability to look after his/her own personal, legal and financial affairs. That's why *these things should be discussed* and planned as soon as possible. Remember the passport example?

Death and loss of mental capacity aren't the exclusive domain of the elderly.

Every day *people of all ages die or lose mental capacity*. We don't control the timing of accidents, illness or our passing. The day will come when we'll no longer be capable of providing for the people we love, even if we can still care for ourselves. The consequences of these events are too important to leave to chance. It's even worth putting funeral arrangements in place in advance, to save your grieving family the burden of organising a funeral and burial/cremation when you pass away.

Fortunately, you can plan for that time and put structures in place now to help secure your future and that of your family. A well-structured estate plan can give great peace of mind that you will be cared for if you can no longer look after yourself and that your loved ones will be provided for as you intended.

A **checklist of estate planning issues** you might consider and (as appropriate) discuss with family members, or your professional advisors can be found in **Schedule I** to this book.

A good estate planning lawyer should have extensive experience across all or most of these areas and understand the complexities involved. S/he can help assess your personal circumstances, assist you to write an appropriate estate plan and work cooperatively with your other professional advisors such as your accountant, financial planner and insurance adviser to cover off on issues that are beyond a lawyer's professional discipline.

Engaging such a lawyer ensures that you will have an integrated plan that covers all the bases. And it needn't stop there. A good lawyer can help ensure that your dependants are looked after through whatever circumstances should arise over their lifetime.

The objectives of broad-based family estate planning are usually:

1. **Ongoing financial support of**
   - Spouse
   - Children, other relatives,
   - Other dependants or organisations you support
2. **Accumulation of wealth for**
   - Lifestyle needs
   - Retirement
3. **Structures for asset protection against**
   - Business risks
   - Family risks
4. **Continued control if you lose capacity**
   - Legal and financial attorney
   - Health and welfare attorney
   - Advanced health care directives
5. **Coordinated strategies for asset distribution**
   - Business assets: company, partnership, trust
   - Trust assets, Superannuation, Life Insurance
   - Personal assets
   - Digital assets

Estate planning is a three-part process involving:

I. **Identification of assets** and who owns them (individual, company, trust, joint)
2. **Identification of potential risks**
3. **Design and implementation of a plan taking into account items I and 2**

Refer to Schedule 2 of the book for a more comprehensive outline of this process.

WHERE DO YOU BEGIN THE PLANNING JOURNEY?

Let's begin now... I promise it won't hurt (too much).

QUESTIONS	Are your estate planning needs straightforward? Do you have family or financial circumstances that require special attention? Do you know where to start? Do you have someone you can turn to for assistance? What will it involve?

Most people avoid estate planning because it's all too daunting. They simply don't know where to begin. Let's see if I can give you a head start. Answer these questions 'yes' or 'no'.

- Do any beneficiaries suffer from an intellectual disability or have special needs?
- Do any beneficiaries have problems managing money?
- Do you have a blended family (children from a prior relationship)?
- Are any beneficiaries facing potential bankruptcy or liquidation?
- Are any beneficiaries facing a potential relationship breakdown?
- Do any beneficiaries have an addiction problem?
- Do you wish to create a life interest in property or make a gift conditional?

- Do you have a self-managed superannuation fund, company or trust?
- Do you conduct/own a business?
- Do you wish to leave a child out of your Will?
- Have you any unresolved family law, property or maintenance issues?
- Do you have overseas assets or non-resident beneficiaries?
- Are any beneficiaries overseas residents?
- Are you concerned about the taxation consequences of death?

If you answered 'no' to these questions, your planning requirements are relatively uncomplicated, and you should proceed to make a Will, an Enduring Power of Attorney and Enduring Guardianship without delay.

If you answered 'yes' to any of these questions, then you have identified an issue requiring specific planning attention. The longer you leave these matters, the harder it can be to address them in your plans. If you answered 'yes' to any of the questions concerning asset protection, vulnerable beneficiaries tax issues then you'd be wise to include chapter nine (Testamentary Trusts) in your perusal of this book.

Regardless of your answers, by undertaking this short exercise you have already begun the planning process, as you have identified any issues that require special attention so that you can seek the appropriate guidance.

Congratulations!

Now, take the next step and undertake a full succession planning self-assessment. I run a Personal Estate Planning and Business Succession

Planning practice and offer this assessment without charge and there are no obligations attached.

| ACTION 1 | As a trial run, you might wish to manually complete a shortened version of the Estate Planning Self-Assessment Tool by completing the questionnaire in Schedule 3 to this book. It won't provide you with answers but may help you identify issues you need to address. |

| ACTION 2 | Alternatively visit my website at: *www.rodcunichlawyer.com/forms/* and request a self-assessment form, complete it and send to me or provide it to your local estate planning specialist. |

PROFESSIONAL GUIDANCE

Estate planning isn't complicated, but you can't be expected to know what you don't know.

Most people need some professional guidance to piece together their affairs. Some need a lot.

One of the most difficult things to achieve is choosing appropriate professional advisers to do the job. As mentioned before, that job is often a multidisciplinary task involving a lawyer, financial planner, accountant and insurance adviser. They will combine to identify and coordinate your legal needs along with asset protection, wealth accumulation, taxation advice, retirement planning and end of life matters. Most importantly, good advice is tailored to what matters most to you.

1. **Check** your adviser's experience, qualifications and reputation (ask for testimonials from satisfied clients – check they aren't family!).
2. Get a **comprehensive breakdown** of what's included in the service and what isn't.
3. **Familiarise yourself** in advance with the issues you need to address and evaluate your adviser on how s/he addresses each of these (the estate planning self-assessment tool referred to above will be of great assistance here).
4. Find out upfront how **fees** are calculated – and ask for a fixed fee quotation.
5. Ensure your lawyer, financial planner, accountant and other advisors are happy to work together **cooperatively**. If any of them are hesitant to deal with the others, replace the uncooperative one – s/he doesn't have your best interests at heart.

Ben, aged 21, died in a work accident at a construction site in Canberra. There was a $200,000 workers compensation payout. He had no Will. His girlfriend claimed all his assets including the money claiming she had lived with Ben for eight months. Ben's family denied this and his mother claimed his property under the ACT intestacy laws. A court case followed. Ben's Mum is reported to have said she fought the case because of the principle, not the money. In particular she wanted Ben's keepsakes – some personal items, a gold chain and cross. The court however made a finding that Ben's girlfriend was financially dependent on him so she received all his property including the workers compensation payout and personal keepsakes that his Mum wanted returned to the family. His mother was so devastated that she created a website to encourage young people to prepare a will: www.willityourway.com.

NON-ESTATE ASSETS – THOSE THAT BY-PASS YOUR WILL

You may hold **investments** in your own name, through a superannuation fund, through a company or through a family trust.

If you own assets personally, when you die your executor gathers the assets together and takes control of them. The executor holds them on trust until your debts are paid and then distributes the assets in accordance with your Will. Whilst in the executor's control these assets are referred to as a person's deceased estate. But not all assets you control are actually owned by you personally and therefore may not become part of your estate and may not be controlled by your Will.

For example, your superannuation death benefit may go directly to your spouse or minor children, as might your life insurance proceeds or your half-share in a jointly owned property, shares or bank accounts. These items often go direct to a person without ever becoming part of your estate. That is, they bypass your estate and aren't controlled by your Will.

If you control a trust that owns investments or other assets, the trust will continue to own those assets after you pass away. To ensure the trust and its assets pass to your desired beneficiary you need to know who will inherit control of your trust and how. This requires a close examination of the terms of the trust deed and often requires documents to be prepared in tandem to your Will. I explain this further a little later in this chapter.

Questions:

1. Do I have any assets that won't form part of my estate and are therefore outside the control of my Will?
2. Is my current situation the best arrangement for my dependants and me or should I change my arrangements, so my Will controls these assets?
3. Can I change my current arrangements so that one or more of these assets is controlled by my Will?

Consider:

- Assets held in a family trust or a company don't form part of your estate. They can't be directly dealt with by your Will. *Control* of the trust or company might be passed on by your Will, but equally the future control of these entities may be dictated by a trust deed, constitution or shareholders agreement.

- Other assets may or may not pass through your estate, depending on whether you want them to or not. For example, superannuation death benefits, life insurance proceeds and interests in jointly owned property. You must determine whether they go through your estate or bypass your estate and go directly to another person. You must know the current situation with these assets and make changes if required to satisfy your wishes.

The complexities don't enable me to elaborate on all these options and variables in this book. If you don't know the pros and cons of each option, don't guess, the outcome could be the opposite of what you want. Following are some important insights into a few of the more common issues you may face.

| OPTIONAL ACTION | *(subject to obtaining expert advice)* Make relatively minor changes to the way you manage these assets so that they are then controlled by the terms of your Will. |

A LITTLE MORE ABOUT TRUSTS

Trusts are complicated things, the workings of which are little understood by many people who have them. Putting aside the technical legal issues of legal and beneficial ownership and the role of a trustee – in effect *a trust owns assets and holds them on behalf of beneficiaries*.

- You can't pass on these assets in your Will – as you don't own them (the trust owns them).
- You can however pass on *control* of the trust and the assets it holds.

Whether you can pass on control of a trust is determined by the terms of the trust deed and often, but not always, by your Will. There are usually options and different methods you can use to pass on the control of a trust while you're alive or when you die. The critical first step is to learn what happens to control of your trust when you lose mental capacity or die. Do you know? Have you got it covered? Read on as I begin to demystify the basics for you.

Selecting the best option in your circumstances is a planning issue for you to address.

Again, ignoring the technical legal structure of a trust, **a trust** is in effect a legal entity. Someone must manage it – the trustee. Quite often a company looks after the day-to-day control of the assets. It might be a share portfolio or properties, and the beneficiaries are 'all family members'. The trustee is commonly a company controlled by the parents, and when the parents pass away the shares in the company will pass to beneficiaries nominated in the Will.

Most trust deeds nominate a person called an 'appointor', who is the ultimate controller of the trust as s/he can remove and replace the trustee. The ability to replace a trustee isn't an asset, it's a power. The appointor has the power to hire and fire the trustee, so by default the appointor is the ultimate controller of the trust and its assets as the appointor dictates who the trustee is. The appointor can be a beneficiary, another company or an individual. It can be anybody you choose.

It may be that you simply want to pass control to your children equally. You can pass the power of appointor to your children equally, and they'll have to jointly make decisions.

That option may sound ideal, but it means throwing all siblings (and by default – their partners) into a decision-making melting pot. If there's a dispute, watch out! Their partners will have a say simply because most people listen to their partners. Furthermore, if one of your children dies and appoints his or her partner as the executor and beneficiary of their estate, then it's likely that the partner will end up being one of these appointors. How do the in-laws get on?

If this were to occur and disputes arose they'd end up having to consult a specialist litigation lawyer to attempt to unravel the mess.

The takeaway message here is to think about the best way to pass on control and to whom, and then properly document your wishes to ensure they're carried out. No bonus points for guessing that a free or cheap Will won't address these issues.

The starting point in every case is to **read the trust deed** and understand how it deals with the role of appointor and the succession of that role when the initial appointor passes away.

RECOMMENDATION

Recommendation to those who have assets in a trust (usually a business or investments). These are not formal legal clauses and should not be used without expert advice. They simply outline what properly prepared clauses can achieve.

First: 'My Executor is to pass control of my trust to one or as few of my beneficiaries as is possible...', and

Second: '... when the Executor is distributing assets from the estate, s/he is to treat any benefit received outside the estate – such as control of the trust – as if it were a distribution from the estate and adjust the distribution from the estate accordingly', and

Third: a clause to the effect that '...my Executor shall ensure that in addressing the first two points, s/he achieve my overriding desire to achieve an equal distribution of my total wealth taking into account my estate and non-estate assets'.

In that way, control of the trust may be passed to one child to the exclusion of the others, if that's appropriate. So, if the estate says 'I give everybody an equal benefit' – you give one of your children control of the trust, and to the others you give a greater portion of your estate assets. That's often a better outcome than the children inheriting equal control over the trust and then having disputes over how it is managed.

It's not a DIY task though as this type of adjustment clause requires careful integration into a succession plan and, like any tool, can be dangerous in the hands of an inexperienced person.

Example: $3 million in total wealth to be divided among three children. There's $1 million in a family trust and $2 million in the estate. One sibling could be given $1 million from the estate, the second sibling $1 million from the estate, and the third could be given control of the trust. So, number three gets nothing from the estate, but s/he controls the $1 million in the trust and the other two get an equal share out of the estate. If you look at the overall wealth of the deceased, one of them gets part of their inheritance by taking over the trust and the other two get a greater portion the estate assets, but across the whole of the deceased person's total wealth (estate and non-estate assets), it's shared equally.

Cautionary Note: Without forward planning some people load up a lot of assets into a trust, so that if one child gets a control of this trust, there's not enough money left in the estate for the other two to get an equal share of the overall wealth. That means the appointor role must be passed to two or more children. It's like throwing people together into partnership. If they get on famously, it's likely to work. Typically, however, jointly controlling a trust brings about disharmony, as individual interests and needs differ with the passage of time. One may want cash to buy a home; another may want to retain the commercial investments held by the trust, as they return a good income, and so on.

In many situations a deceased person throws multiple beneficiaries, all with different interests, into control of a trust simply because s/he hasn't thought through the potential risks.

Having gotten on extremely well throughout their lives, doesn't mean siblings won't argue over an inheritance. It's not a temperament-thing, as tensions are often caused by outside influences – like their financial circumstances or their partners.

They all have different financial circumstances (some may need a lump sum, others might prefer income), meaning they won't all want to do the same thing with their portion and it may not be possible to satisfy all their needs. So, keep them apart, don't foist them into the same (boxing) ring.

Even when they have thought through these issues some clients say 'I'll be dead, so I don't care. It's their problem to sort out'. Like all planning choices, it's yours to make, but make sure you consider all factors and make an informed decision.

Here's one example of how things can go wrong:

*Tom is one of three children who inherit assets from their parent's estate. Most of their wealth was tied up in their family trust. The trust owns a large warehouse that is leased to a long-term tenant. Each child received an equal number of shares in the trustee company, each was appointed a director of the trustee company and each was appointed as joint appointor of the trust. Seems fair and equitable doesn't it? Then the black cloud descended. Tom wanted a lump sum from the trust to pay a deposit on a new home his wife was keen on. The trust couldn't provide a lump sum without selling the warehouse or borrowing the money. Tom's siblings were happy with the income stream from the trust and refused to sell the warehouse or borrow money. A dispute broke out and Tom's siblings turned on him and began to out-vote him as a director. It became so bitter that the siblings stopped all money flowing to Tom and took his **notional share**. He couldn't do anything about it as he was in the minority. Tom's wife left him due to the disappointment and stress, and then the trust was dragged into a family law property dispute with Tom's wife who claimed a share of the trust assets. A sorry mess all round.*

JOINTLY OWNED ASSETS

Some of the problems associated with passing on joint control of trusts also arises with jointly owned assets.

TO SELL, OR NOT TO SELL

Julian and Brett's parents never imagined their boys could argue over anything. They had an ideal sibling relationship. Things being so smooth between them, they left them a block of flats jointly.

But their financial circumstances were very different. Consequently, Julian wanted to sell the investment properties because he needed the money to buy a house. And Brett, who had a higher income, was happy to keep receiving rental income. He didn't want to sell. He didn't need or want a capital sum.

Julian and Brett were at loggerheads, both with equally genuine, but different, interests in how the assets should be managed.

They have been advised that they own the flats as joint tenants and that if either die, the survivor automatically owns all the flats. Their wives aren't happy.

How do you deal with that?

TENANTS IN COMMON

Jointly-owned properties must be given special consideration in your estate planning. If two parties own property together it can be problematic if one wants to sell and the other doesn't.

Unless you want your interest to automatically transfer to the other co-owner on your death rather than pass to your estate, you need to ensure it's owned as 'tenants in common' rather than as joint tenants. If owned as 'joint tenants' ownership automatically passes to the survivor on death.

CO-OWNER AGREEMENT

Two or more tenants-in-common (co-owners) can enter a simple agreement where they agree that if one wants out then the other must either purchase the interest or join with the co-owner to sell the whole property. That doesn't happen automatically. To make that happen, you need to put a legal agreement in place.

That is, if someone wants to cash in their lot, they have to offer it first to the other party (or parties). If the others aren't prepared to buy their interest, then the whole lot must be sold and divided up in proportion to their ownership percentages.

That's the sort of thing that you need to see a lawyer about.

Firstly, to have the problem explained. And secondly, to do the documentation.

DEADLOCK

If one party wants to sell an asset and the other doesn't, then in the absence of agreement, there's a deadlock. Nothing happens. That applies to company shares as well as real estate. **Either party can block the sale.**

Land, however, is different. You can do something with land. You can apply to the court and the court can appoint a trustee over the whole of the land. The trustee then sells it, and after costs of sale, the trustee will divide the profit. That requires a costly court application. The cost of the trustee doing his/her job is also high.

A written agreement before the problem arises, is much simpler and more straightforward than struggling through all the above. Both parties can write an agreement that says, 'if either of us wants to get out of it, I'll offer to sell to you'. Should the other party decline, they can negotiate a minimum acceptance price – using the services of a valuer.

Where company shares are involved things are even more difficult in the absence of an agreement as the courts have very limit scope to intervene.

PROTECTING BENEFICIARIES FROM THEMSELVES

Just about every family has a cross to bear. Whether it's a dysfunctional child, a family member with some kind of addiction (i.e. alcohol, drugs, online shopping or gambling), a spendthrift, a poor money manager, someone who's manipulated by their partner or a child with a disability. The outcome is the same – emotional and financial stress surrounding the planning process.

Parents have come to me with concerns that a family member is likely to squander the inheritance they'd like to leave them. Sometimes they want to cut them out entirely as the inheritance will only make existing problems worse. On occasions it's tempting to agree. However, there may be options that fall between the two extremes of leaving money with no strings attached and leaving nothing.

If you're concerned that any inheritance you leave your offspring might be wasted away, here are a few ideas to consider:

1. Place the inheritance in a safe environment

If you doubt your child will make sound decisions about spending their inheritance you can put those decisions in the hands of someone else. You can leave the money in a trust and appoint a competent and caring person to manage the funds for the benefit of your child.

Your child will get the benefit of using assets in the trust and perhaps enjoy the benefits of an income stream. But they never get to spend (or squander) the capital.

These types of arrangements are many and varied so can be tailored to suit your circumstances.

2. Instalments and annuities

People sometimes grow out of their shortcomings. If you're hopeful that maturity will bring a change of their behaviour, you can prepare a Will that staggers the inheritance payments. For example, one-third at age 25, another third at age 35 and the balance at age 40.

Alternatively, instalment payments could be paid annually. Along similar lines, you could establish an annuity (a contract with an insurance company that obligates the company to make payments to a beneficiary). Annuities are often used to provide retirement income, but you can also direct payments to a child. You can arrange either for regular payments of a set amount for a certain period. Or you can arrange for variable payments that depend on the size of the investment premium.

Again, the structures are flexible and can be tailored to fit.

3. Establish incentives

Incentive trusts are designed to reward the behaviour you want and discourage what you don't want. You can arrange for payments to be conditional upon the child achieving specific goals. For example, attending university, getting a job or having a family. It may also go as far as to include behavioural modification programs – where relevant – like completing an alcohol rehab program or staying drug-free.

These types of arrangement have complications because the trustee will be required to make a personal assessment or obtain expert's opinion. Making this type of arrangement work as you wish requires a clear set of guidelines.

Care must also be exercised to ensure you don't go too far and create a situation where the courts will overturn your wishes because they provide inadequate provision for the person, are against public policy or simply can't work. There is a balance to be struck, and each case is dependent on the circumstances and individuals involved. Again, it's not a DIY challenge.

CONTROL BEYOND THE GRAVE

People can leave assets to trusts (rather than individuals) and appoint third parties – such as accountants or other professionals – to manage the trusts for the benefit of beneficiaries. The people managing the trusts (trustees) can be given specific instructions through the Will about how to best manage the assets.

NOTE ▶ *In this way people can rule beyond the grave.*

There are many types of trusts that can be created by Will:
- Trust that appoint the beneficiary as the controller of a trust that holds their own inheritance so that they can protect it against third parties and to take advantage of special taxation benefits
- Trust that appoint third parties to manage a beneficiary's inheritance because the beneficiary is incapable of doing so themselves because of lack of mental capacity, drug or gambling addiction or other inability to manage money
- Trust that simply facilitate the deceased's desire to rule beyond the grave because the willmaker wanted it that way

Refer to chapter nine – Testamentary trusts for specific details.

PERSONAL EFFECTS

Big disputes are often caused by small items of little financial value. Items of sentimental value, such as memorabilia, photographs or 'Dad's favourite watch' are often not specifically gifted to an individual by the Will.

I once had two siblings litigate over control of their mother's estate (they were both executors and the only beneficiaries) because they couldn't agree on who would receive one small item of furniture which had negligible commercial value but lots of sentimental value. They spent their inheritance fighting each other in the courts, neither wanted the other to get anything from the estate.

Their dislike of each other escalated at about the same rate as the legal fees mounted up. Or perhaps, more likely, it happened the other way around — sibling rivalry and associated high emotion make volatile fuel to feed ugly disputes.

To avoid this, some people choose to write out a list in their Will that says, 'Johnny's having my antique clock; and Mary's having my engagement ring...' and they go through and list everything in the house. That's one way of doing it, and the most legally enforceable. It can also result in our more senior clients continuously changing their Wills as family members fall in and out of favour, or as items are broken or thrown out.

A compromise is to make mention in your Will that if you leave a list of gifts with your Will, you wish your executors to do their best to distribute the gifts in accordance with that list. It's not binding on the executors (as a list in the Will would be) but it does give the executors formal guidance and authority to deal with the listed items. *That way the list can be updated as often as required without having to formally rewrite the Will.* This option however doesn't overcome sibling rivalry if they're also the executors.

Another common option is to include in your Will a clause saying that each child (from eldest to youngest) can select one item and then the next in line selects an item and so on (around and around) until all items are selected or rejected.

In cases where people have been partnered for long enough to have acquired most of their things together, these items are treated as being jointly owned unless there is some reason to attribute ownership to one or the other. So, when one partner dies the surviving partner automatically owns it all, without going through the Will. Generally speaking, that's what happens.

There are some exceptions though. Sometimes it's really 'mine' not 'ours'. For example, where someone has a hobby in which their partner has no interest. In my case it's cycling and photography... but let's suppose it's golf. Technically speaking it might be difficult or impossible to establish whether these items are legally owned by the golfer alone, or jointly owned with the non-golfing partner.

It's common however, for such items to be treated by partners as being 'owned' by one or the other, regardless of how they were acquired. Quite often a person will leave such items to a particular person (usually a son/daughter, niece/nephew or friend) who shares that interest. A mother will often leave her jewellery to one (or more) of her daughters and will actually specify who gets which item. And a father will traditionally leave his vintage car that needs restoring to one of his sons – often upsetting his daughter-in-law in the process who will lose her husband to a new hobby.

The Will also needs to specify whether the value of the specific gift items is to be ignored or to be taken into account when determining 'equality' between beneficiaries.

People who are preparing their Will should consider, 'what's the value of those items of memorabilia in the beneficiary's hands?' If it only has sentimental value, that's fine. But if it's an item that has some commercial value then it may need extra consideration.
Suppose it's something that can be published, like a war diary. Such an item has sentimental value, but also a potentially added value as a published book. In the hands of the beneficiary it's much more

valuable than your collection of detective novels that someone else receives. It's your choice to ignore the actual value of items, and many do... **But:** make it a *conscious decision* by thinking through these issues and addressing fairness, if required, to balance things up.

Also, if the item is valuable ask yourself, is it to be treated as part of a child's share of the balance of the estate? Or is it to be treated as a gift which is in addition to their equal share of the balance of my estate?

Fairness doesn't necessarily mean equal value, but what you view as fair may be seen as unfair by your beneficiaries *— so talk to them about it before you leave behind a ticking time bomb*. Explain your reasoning; it could (and most often does) avoid a family feud once you leave the scene.

If you have two children and you leave to each a vacant block of land and;
- One builds a block of flats on the property and sells it for a fortune;
- While the other who didn't have the money to develop it can only ever sell it as a vacant block of land, for minimum profit...

... that's just tough luck. *You* treated them equally. Their circumstances didn't.

You can't determine what happens to property once you pass it on. It's the beneficiary's responsibility.

But is that always the case?
Answer. No.

WHAT DOES 'EQUAL' MEAN?

Problems usually occur when the second partner dies. This is because a lot more people can dispute the Will. In many instances, the parents simply leave instructions to 'divide my estate equally'. But unless there's some description of what 'equally' means, that's almost asking for trouble because (to make sense of the estate) the executor must ask the question: 'what does *equal* mean?'

• Does that mean equal **financial value**? (Should we have every item valued?)
• Does it mean equal in **number** of items? (If I get one, you get one.)
• And when you've worked that out, ask – does a cutlery set count as one item? Or is each individual piece a single item?
• Or, does it refer to equal **sentimental value**? (How do we measure that?)

If you don't want to specify which item goes to whom, you could write something like this into the will: 'I leave all my goods and chattels to my three children. The eldest can choose the first item; the second child has second choice; the third child has third choice... (and a set of anything is to be treated as a single item!)' and so they continue in that rotation.

Or, you could do what my grandmother did (and I'm sure lots of other grandmothers did too!). She stuck coloured stickers on the back of each item on which she wrote the initials of the person whom she wanted to receive it. The notes had no legal effect but at least her executors had some guide as to who should get what. Although I've always wondered if someone may have swapped a few stickers around. I wouldn't recommend my grandmother's approach, but more than one granny has ignored my advice in the past and I'm sure others will choose to do so in the future.

Below is a copy of the note (it's not a formal will) my grandmother left taped to the inside of her grandfather clock. Not only did she leave it to me – she created a life interest for my mother to use the clock whilst she was alive. Mum is still well but I have the clock already – Dad couldn't cope with the chiming!

Understanding Wills and Estate Planning

STEP-CHILDREN AND SECOND PARTNER ISSUES

In the situation where the first partner dies, the administration of their Will usually progresses reasonably smoothly. This is because the deceased usually leaves everything to the other partner, who now has a houseful of furniture, memorabilia, trinkets, knick-knacks, etc. Of course, that may upset some relatives such as the survivor's stepchildren (the deceased children by an earlier partner), but generally people don't like to disrupt an existing household.

But don't assume things will be smooth sailing. In these circumstances step-children often feel vulnerable as they feel their inheritance is disappearing into the coffers of their step parent. There are numerous legal strategies you can implement to protect their future inheritance once their step parent passes away.

Mutual Wills Agreements

One such strategy is the use of a mutual wills agreement ('MWA')

Couples (married or de facto) often wish to leave their estate to each and then, on the death of the survivor, have their combined estate divided between their respective families. Typically, this occurs with blended families where there are children from prior relationships.

Each party relies on the survivor to 'do the right thing'.

Generally, there are no restrictions on a person changing their Will. When the first passes away, the surviving partner can alter their Will. This may result in a new Will that does not reflect their current shared intentions. For example, the surviving partner may alter their Will to remove step children as beneficiaries in order to favour their own children or a new life partner. With all the best intentions, circumstances change, and it is impossible to predict what might happen in the future, particularly if the surviving partner is under the influence of third parties or their affairs are in the hands of a person who holds their Enduring Power of Attorney.

How do you ensure that your property ends up in the hands of your preferred beneficiaries, whilst allowing your partner to have use of your assets whilst they are still alive?

There is no single or simple solution.

One estate planning tool designed to help minimise this type of risk is an agreement you enter into with your partner to the effect that neither of you will change the broad intentions in your Will after the first dies. Such an agreement is called a Mutual Wills Agreement ('MWA'). A MWA is a legally binding document and serves as a mechanism to reduce the chances of the surviving partner changing their mind with respect to their Will.

Obligations of parties to Mutual Wills Agreements

MWAs give rise to obligations on the part of the surviving partner. The surviving partner becomes the trustee of the estate for the beneficiaries named in the Wills. The surviving partner is bound by the agreement.

If either partner changes their Will contrary to the agreement, the courts may intervene to enforce the agreement.

Breaches and Remedies: It is important that the beneficiaries are informed of the existence of the agreement, as they have the right to enforce the agreement. If the surviving partner has unreasonably exhausted all the assets of the deceased, beneficiaries may sue for breach of contract.

Shortcomings of Mutual Wills Agreement: MWA have the following shortcomings:
1. A MWA cannot prevent a Will being challenged under the relevant state or territory legislation.
2. Changes in circumstances may occur after the MWA been executed which result in the survivor being disadvantaged. A remarriage of the surviving partner can also complicate the operation of the agreement.
3. The survivor may deliberately attempt to frustrate the operation of a MWA by depleting estate assets or changing the way they are owned.
4. The survivor's power of attorney may deliberately attempt to frustrate the operation of a MWA by depleting estate assets or changing the way they are owned.

Tailor Enduring Power of Attorney: The parties would be well advised to also expressly restrict the powers of their Enduring Power of Attorney to prohibit their Attorney using their powers to 'get-around' the terms of a MWA.

Shortcomings such as disadvantage, depletion of assets, changes to ownership structures and lack of maintenance of the assets can be minimised with a well-drawn MWA, however MWAs are not an absolute guarantee of certainty. They work best in conjunction with other strategies if they are available.

Remarriage: It is important to note that remarriage will not change the obligations under the agreement, but remarriage will automatically terminate an existing Will. The survivor should see a lawyer to obtain advice should they remarry.

Conclusion: A MWA is one 'tool' you can use to help achieve your wishes. Although a Mutual Wills Agreement is sometimes the best solution, they are imperfect. The agreement will minimise the risk of your wishes being avoided but does not guarantee protection.

There are other strategies that can be used in conjunction with, or as an alternate to, a MWA to help preserve your testamentary intentions.

DIGITAL ASSETS

With the Computer Age there comes a new type of asset – digital assets. *What digital assets do you own?* For example, do you own your online digital library? No, you don't. What about all the photographs on Facebook, Flickr or that type of service provider? In most cases their *Terms and Conditions* will say they own it. But few people read the terms and conditions, and even fewer understand them. Once the service provider knows you've died, many will cut off access to your account and close it whilst others offer other options if you authorise your executor to deal with them on your behalf.

Music and movie accounts are usually shut down by the service provider. Many website service providers work on the basis that once you die so does your account. That music library may have cost thousands, but access to the account cannot be passed on, as with CDs and LP records. When the provider finds out about a death – the account disappears! If you're lucky you might access a copy of data from the computer's hard drive or back up drive but check the terms of the provider's licence as use by anyone other than the account owner is likely to be unlawful.

This is a rapidly changing area due to the public demanding more control. Governments in some countries are legislating to allow executors greater rights over a deceased person's digital assets. These developments will eventually reach Australia's shores, in fact we're already beginning to enjoy the benefit of some changes forced on online providers.

For example, if your Will authorises and directs your executor to deal with your online digital assets some providers are now allowing:
- continued access to accounts for a limited time,
- accounts to be memorialised, or
- all content removed from the internet.

Question: Memorialised? What's That?

Answer: When you die, the website manager (service provider) leaves your online content 'up there' and freezes the account, therefore confirmed friends can look at it in the future for a specific period or perhaps forever. The site can't be accessed by the general public however.

Some websites such as Facebook allow pages to be memorialised in a way that enables family and friends ('confirmed friends') to access the account and add new posts and photographs to the account, in memory of the deceased.

Each service provider's terms and conditions differ, and they're continuously changing. It's worth checking your status, as your digital assets may or may not be part of your estate that can be managed by your executor. But remember, even if your account managers don't currently play ball, their policies are changing as rapidly as technology itself. **You should seriously consider including a digital assets clause in your Will,** so that it can be acted upon if, at the time of your death, it's possible to control your online and other digital assets.

Recommendation: catalogue your digital assets and access codes, store in a safe place (with your Will perhaps) and instruct your executor or Enduring Power of Attorney what you want done with them. If you need help, just ask me or your local estate planning specialist.

Future option: When you open an account with a social media website, for example, instead of opening it up in your own name, open it in the name of a company acting as trustee of a trust. When you die, your login and password details may be passed to someone nominated in your Will — and this person can continue to log on because *the trust is the owner of the license, not the individual* and the trust lives on.

Is that against the law? No, because the licensee is still alive (it's a company). Is there a public service of this nature available in Australia? At the date of writing — no. Such companies do exist in the USA so it's probably only a matter of time before they appear in Australia. So, watch this space.

OTHER 'VIRTUAL' OR 'DIGITAL' RELATED ISSUES

It's important your executor is made aware of all your accounts, so they can be dealt with. Executors often haven't undertaken the role before and aren't aware of the duties and obligations imposed on them by the law, so don't keep these details a secret — unless of course there is good reason to do so.

LinkedIn will stop 'Invitations to Follow' a person once advised that the person has passed away. But someone with authority must ask and provide evidence of death. I recently met a chap who still gets invitations to follow his best friend who died two years ago. It upsets him every time the invitation appears, but he has no authority to put a stop to it occurring.

As for bank accounts, betting accounts, shopping accounts and the like, I'd recommend all details be removed from a deceased person's accounts ASAP. There is the risk of being hacked and no one noticing it. But that's not the only problem. Too many of us, myself included, ask our internet browsers to 'remember' our passwords. Add that to the fact that our login ID is often easy to guess (our email address or another obvious identifier) and anyone can access our accounts and have a spending spree by simply turning on our computer, tablet or smart phone. Abuse of an account-linked credit card will eventually come to the notice of an executor, but as they say... by that stage the horse has bolted.

3. Retain control beyond your mental capacity

People associate estate planning with events that happen after – not before – they die, such as the distribution of their estate. But loss of mental and/or physical capacity is a real risk that people face, and a risk that increases with age.

That's why you should make arrangements to cover a situation where you're still alive but can no longer manage your own affairs. That's part of the planning process. It's too late once you begin talking to the pixies at the back of the garden.

ACTION Ask yourself these questions:

1. If I should lose the ability to manage my legal and financial affairs, who would act in my best interests?
2. If I were declared incapable of handling my estate, what would happen to my property if I made no advance arrangements?
3. What can I do to ensure my affairs are managed by someone competent, someone I trust?

ENDURING POWER OF ATTORNEY (EPOA)

A General Power of Attorney ceases to operate if you lose mental capacity. An ***Enduring*** Power of Attorney continues to operate after you lose mental capacity. In all other respects they are the same.

If you lose your ability to reason, someone else must manage your finances. It needs to be:

(a) Someone you trust

(b) Someone who understands your wishes

(c) Someone who won't mismanage or abuse your wealth.

With a few very limited exceptions, legally, the appointed Attorney can only use their power — including the spending of money in the accounts — for the benefit of the person who appoints them.

Your Attorney has the power to use their power without consulting you — even if you still have capacity.

Example: Mum and Dad are in a nursing home and their POA says, 'I'm spending all my time helping my parents, so I'll use their money to buy a car in my own name, because it's to their benefit that I run them around and I'm sure they'd want me to own it'. That's the sort of area where one may wonder who really gets the benefit?

Carmel is a dentist with a wealthy mother who suffered from dementia. All three siblings were appointed joint-guardians. Carmel and one sibling agreed that their mother should be kept in a manner to which she had been accustomed. The other thought it was too expensive and that the cost would significantly eat into their future inheritance. She voted for a cheap nursing home.

'She doesn't know what's happening anyway...', said this sibling, '...so it doesn't actually matter!' After a family squabble plus legal advice, Carmel's side prevailed. She said, 'Mum deserves the best, she's always been good to us'.

However, what if there hadn't been three siblings? What if the guardianship of Carmel's mother had been left totally in the hands of the one who didn't want to spend the money? That can happen, if you pick the wrong person.

You can easily address these issues to suit yourself before they arise.

ACTION

Execute an Enduring Power of Attorney, appointing one or more trusted people to manage your legal and financial affairs on your behalf. Tell them how you want your affairs managed. Remember, people don't know what they don't know, so tell them. Don't leave them guessing.

Caution should be exercised in your choice of people, as these documents can be used to take financial advantage of the elderly. You might appoint one or more people – perhaps your partner, close friend, child/children or a trusted professional adviser, such as your lawyer. You can also appoint backups if (for some reason) your first choice can't act.

This simple document enables you to appoint someone to lawfully act on your behalf if you're unable or don't wish to make any decisions about legal and financial matters.

Not only do you select **who** looks after your affairs, you can also direct the person you appoint on **how** you wish the power to be exercised.

ACTION

Amend your Enduring Power of Attorney document to expressly include directions and restrictions.

Beware of elder abuse

In this instance, I cannot over stress the need for caution. Firstly, the person granted EPOA doesn't have to announce it. I've seen examples of one sibling exercising Power of Attorney without the knowledge of the other siblings.

It can happen quite often because one sibling puts pressure on the parents. The sibling is always calling on the parents and convinces ageing Mum or Dad that because they turn up more often, they're the one who should have control. I don't mean to sound sinister. I'm sure most people drop in on Mum and Dad for the best of reasons, but some have used emotional strings to convince their parents to grant them EPOA. And people who are old and frail often find it hard to say no.

Abuse of these documents is common. You need to be alert. Refer to chapter four 'Dismantling with Dignity', for more information on this issue.

Warning: Powers of Attorney are easy to misuse – sometimes fraudulently – sometimes naively. They often facilitate 'elder abuse', that is, they are used to financially advance the attorney and disadvantage the elderly person who has appointed them. So, on the one hand they are an essential planning tool but on the other hand must be prepared with caution as they can be used to cause great hardship. Choosing the right 'attorney/s' becomes a major consideration.

How can a granny flat evolve into elder abuse?

It is common for a child to offer to care for their parent if the parents sell their home and use the money to build a granny flat or extra rooms at the child's home. The offer is usually made with the very best of intentions. Unfortunately, the wheels all too often fall off these arrangements because all the parent's wealth is now tied up in the child's property. For example, what happens if the child gets divorced and their property is sold as part of the property settlement. The parents lose their home and their money. Or, what if they need to move into a care facility as they are too frail to be cared for at home, but there is no money available to pay the bond or daily fees.

ACTION — If you wish to take up a child's offer to care for you in this type of arrangement then 'lend' the child the money and document the loan. Don't give the money to them.

And if you don't have an Enduring Power of Attorney ...?

Not having the Enduring Power of Attorney in place, means you're handing the management of your affairs to the courts.

With no such document, your family (or healthcare provider) would have to apply to a tribunal or the courts to appoint a **financial manager**. This costs money and can result in delaying the making of urgent decisions. And of course, you would have no say in who's appointed, or what they do with you or your assets. Once you've lost mental capacity through accident or the ageing process it's out of your control.

HIS THREE SONS

Harry is a self-made man who worked hard all his life and accumulated modest wealth. His wife died shortly after Bill, their third son, was born, and Harry raised him as a sole parent.

Unlike his older brothers who work overseas, Bill left school early and made his living through various pyramid selling schemes. His brothers suggested that Bill was a bit of a rogue. Others said he couldn't be trusted, but his father adored his youngest son and saw things differently.

As he aged, Harry suffered early-onset Alzheimer's. He also lost a lot of physical mobility. Bill took custody of his father who signed guardianship and EPOA documents in his favour, without Bill advising his brothers.

The older brothers returned to discover that Harry now had advanced Alzheimer's and was living in a sub-standard nursing home. Furthermore, Bill had squandered his father's wealth using his EPOA.

By the time all this came to light, Bill had no assets, so the money couldn't be recovered. At their own expense, the older sons transferred their father to a better aged care facility.

WHAT WENT WRONG	In his advancing years, with faltering mind and unable to resist pressure, Harry gave the guardianship and EPOA to an inappropriate person.

It's common for partners to appoint each other to this role. I recommend that you also appoint a backup or substitute Attorney in case your first choice can't fulfil the role.

To appoint an Attorney as an alternative decision maker you must complete a formal Enduring Power of Enduring (known by different names in different jurisdictions).

The lessons:
- Prepare these documents now – while you can still make an informed decision without any undue pressure and maximise the chances of making the right decision.
- Despite the risk of abuse, they are invaluable
- Minimise the risks by only appointing trusted people, preferably more than one jointly so they keep each other honest.

GUARDIANSHIP

While you have the mental capacity, you can do two things:

1. Execute an 'Appointment of Enduring Guardian': by which you appoint someone you know and trust to make health and welfare decisions for you, when you can't do so yourselves. This includes for example, where you live, and,
2. Execute an 'Advanced Health Care Directive' by which you direct your doctors what medical treatment you don't wish to receive when you can no longer decide for yourself.

It's a good plan to do both, but either is better than none. Leaving everything up in the air transfers the burden of decision making to your loved ones. Or worse still, to strangers who have no idea what our wishes might be.

Just as you can appoint someone to make financial and legal decisions on your behalf, you can also appoint someone to make health and welfare decisions if you're unable to do so – decisions such as where you live and the type of medical treatment that you receive.

A guardian literally acts in lieu of the person who has lost the ability to manage his/her life. Once we lose mental capacity others will make decisions for us. But who? And on what basis? Are these the same decisions we would have made for ourselves?

A guardian is supposed to make the best healthcare decisions and will be granted his or her wishes unless someone else in the family applies to a Guardianship Tribunal to intervene. If someone puts them to the test, the guardian needs to satisfy the Guardianship Tribunal that his/her decisions are being made in the best interests of the person in their care. If there are no other family members or interested parties, *tough luck* – you'll get what you're given.

That's why it's important to choose a guardian who understands what you want. You must be satisfied that s/he is prepared to genuinely implement your wishes.

It's common for spouses/partners to appoint each other to this role. I recommend that you also appoint a backup or substitute guardian in case your first choice can't fulfil the role.

To appoint a guardian as an alternative decision maker you must complete a formal *'Appointment of Enduring Guardian'* (known by different names in different jurisdictions).

You require a different document to direct end of life decisions about what medical treatment you wish to refuse. See the next section.

LIVING WILLS OR ADVANCED HEALTH CARE DIRECTIVES

Except in Victoria where there is new legislation allowing for euthanasia in limited circumstances, in Australia, we don't have a right to end our own life, *but every mentally competent adult has a legal right to accept or refuse medical treatment, even if the refusal of that treatment leads to their death.*

There are several terms used to describe the document by which you give directions about medical treatment. They're commonly called 'Living Wills' but are also referred to as 'Advanced Health Care Directives' or simply 'Health Care Directives'.

They all have the same objectives:
- to protect **your right to refuse** unwanted medical treatment,
- to protect **your right to receive** desired medical treatment, and,
- to ensure **you receive relief** from pain and suffering to the maximum extent that is reasonable in the circumstances.

Any medical professional providing treatment contrary to your health care directive is exposed to charges of assault, claims of negligence and/or breach of contract.

Usually these documents stipulate treatment *limitation* preferences, but they may indicate a wish that you want full measures taken to prolong your life, no matter what the treatment.

The medical treatment preferences can include for example:
- preferences influenced by religious or other values and beliefs,
- they can identify living circumstances unacceptable to you arising from dependence on life-sustaining treatment, and,
- direct how far treatment should go when your condition is declared 'terminal', 'incurable' or 'irreversible'.

If you have appointed a guardian, s/he is bound to follow the directions set out in your health care directive. In the absence of a health care directive your guardian has a free hand in deciding what treatment you receive, but not what you can refuse.

In some states and territories these powers are included in the statutory form of their 'power of attorney' documents, so the form and how it must be executed are prescribed by legislation. In others they aren't and have to be separately prepared without reference to any legislative requirements.

4. Dismantle with dignity

It's not just death that brings an end to the family home as we have known it. Thanks to the impact of the ageing process, we often must move out of the family home years before we actually pass away. And we often leave behind many of our personal belongings, as they won't fit in our new abode.

- Do you wish to manage the distribution of your belongings? or
- Place everything in storage and let the executors of your Will deal with it when the time comes?

When it's time to downsize and perhaps move to a hostel or other aged care facility, the family home is usually dismantled. Much of the furniture, household goods and even heritage items (such as photos and memorabilia) are jettisoned simply because there is no space in our next home. Once the time to move out of the family home arrives, it's likely that many of your belongings will be distributed amongst family and friends, given to charities, or sold. This can occur long before you die. And sometimes it occurs quite suddenly, triggered by a health event or accident. How do I know? I have a truck licence (left over from working my way through university) and I often get calls from friends along these lines, 'Mum's just broken her hip and has to relocate. Can you help us move her stuff?'

If you can't retain them, how would you like to distribute all these goodies? Your Will won't help because you'll still be alive. You could place it all in storage and let your executors worry about it, but this costs money and removes from you the joy of giving gifts to friends and family.

If you do have a view about these items, then you need to put a plan into place before an emergency forces the decision on you at a time when you're preoccupied by health issues. And of course, all this should happen before any loss of mental capacity.

In reality, in many cases, 'stuff' just disappears. Big brother turns up and says, 'I was promised that...', while big sister says, 'I was promised this...' Meanwhile the sibling who lives out of town, doesn't really get a look-in. By the time a Will is read there may be no item of value left to distribute. Again, that can create huge disputes. The best way to avoid such problems is to write out a list or designate who's entitled to what.

A legal matter crossed my desk not long ago, where a Mum was in an aged care facility, so one of the siblings slipped over to the old family home and loaded a truck with the furniture and personal effects.

While this was happening, the other siblings turned up and said, 'Stop! This isn't right!'

'I deserve this', said the one with the truck, 'I've been the one looking after Mum over the last five years while you lot only visited her at Christmas!' Then he hopped into the truck and drove off. A puff of black exhaust fumes – gone.

How do you get it back? Technically, the executor of the estate can demand it back. But that involves a court case with siblings, which is why it crossed my desk. In the end, they just let it lie... but the ill-will festers to this day.

The person who drove off wasn't a bad person. They acted in haste and at a time of grief. Their action was completely out of character but once the deed was done, they would not, or could not, back down. It ruined that family's relationships.

DONATIONS, SERVICES AND WOLVES IN SHEEP SKIN COVERS

When sensing the end is near, representatives of some churches, charities and even con artists become quite active in asking for financial contributions. They ask ageing people to donate to various causes, some of which are worthy, others dubious. But frailty may result in the giving of generous gifts that wouldn't have been made in normal circumstances.

Reputable charities and other organisations don't conduct them-selves this way but be alert to the fringe dwellers.

I once had a client approach me and say, 'Mum has always been supportive of her church when they were raising money to help care for the poor and the needy but refused to contribute to their building fund. She's now old and frail and has early onset dementia. I just found out the local pastor convinced her to give a large donation to help build a state-of-the-art high-tech office facility, something she wouldn't have supported if she knew what she was doing... I don't think she really understood what the money was for. She trusts her pastor and I think he took advantage of her. What can we do about it?'

Then of course there are the shonky 'tradesmen' who prey on the elderly selling them services they don't need. Their only skill in many cases is the ability to win confidence so they can extract hard earned wealth. I've seen elderly people talked into a new roof, exterior cladding, re-wiring the home, complete garden refurbishment and roof insulation. In some cases, they did a good job, in others a poor job but in all these cases the work was unnecessary and forced on the elderly.

What can you do to prevent elderly people being ripped off?

Solution: The only real protection is family and caring neighbours. Hopefully, people who are frail or losing their mental facilities have supportive family members and neighbours around them to give them assistance and advice and keep an eye on them. Their children (who have an interest in the future inheritance) need to act as watchdog. If there is no family, these people are really exposed to being exploited. Where there is a regular trickle of donations to a suspect cause, the family members can help bring an end to it.

Whether they can recover any money or not depends on the circumstances. It's hard to prove that these people took advantage. And elderly people, even if conned, often prefer not to accuse churches, charities and others of wrongdoing.

When supporting the elderly, the best protection is to *be alert*. Regularly remind them not to be too trusting. Convince them to defer decision-making about money matters until their family can be consulted. (Do this even if none of them holds Power of Attorney.)

Be on your guard. Perhaps have the elderly relative give trusted people an Enduring Power of Attorney and have them refer all questions about gifts and other payments to their attorney.

In a high-risk situation perhaps use the Enduring Power of Attorney to restrict the elderly person's access to money and credit facilities.

Getting it back: Clawing back money that's already gone can be problematic, but it's not impossible. If you can prove someone used **undue influence** or unconscionable conduct to take advantage of a vulnerable person, then you can undo what they did. Whether it's a sibling who wants a larger slice of the estate or a minister of religion who says 'sign money over to this great cause' – if you can show that the person exercised control or 'undue influence' or 'unconscionable conduct' at a time the person was especially susceptible to influence, then donations and gifts can be clawed back.

PROBLEM

The practical problem is that these situations often involve small sums of money and the cost of recovery simply outweighs the benefit of getting it back.

WHO THE HECK ARE BOB AND JANE?

A lady recently came to me to write her Will. She said, 'When I die I want to leave all my assets to Bob and Jane'.

I said, 'Who are Bob and Jane?'

She replied, 'I want to leave it to my church where they're the current ministers. It's just a small church run from their home'.

I said, 'If you leave it to them personally, then they'll personally own it – not the church. If your wish is to leave it to the church let's find out the legal body involved and leave the money to that entity, not just to individuals personally. Do that and it's likely to end up in the hands of their children'.

She was completely convinced that the best way for her to benefit the church was to leave it to the individuals who ran its local chapter. That's how naïve people can be and how much influence their faith can have on their decisions.

In this case no formal church actually existed, it was simply a group of faithful followers of the minister.

FUNERAL ARRANGEMENTS AND ORGAN DONATION

You can write instructions about whether you wish to be buried or cremated into your Will, but they aren't absolutely binding on your executor/s because it's just an expression of your wish. Executors will usually attempt to fulfil those wishes but they're **not legally bound** to do so. They effectively 'own' your body and it's their call.

PRE-PAYMENT The best way to ensure that you're buried/cremated the way you wish is to pre-pay a funeral. Otherwise, someone could say, 'I'm not going to pay the costs of a grave and a headstone, I'm just going to cremate them and dispose of the ashes'. But if you pre-pay, then it's all set up and done.

Pre-payment also ensures you get the funeral you want at today's prices, even if you live for many years. This can be a huge saving to your estate.

Funeral insurance however, is a very different matter. It can be a very expensive undertaking. For some it works out well and for others it's a financial disaster. You can start paying insurance premiums today but must keep them up until you die – the risk is that you live too long.

Example: pay premiums for eight years, then stop and you'll receive no payout on death to pay for your funeral. On the other hand, many people live long enough that they have paid much more for the insurance premiums than they would pay for a funeral in today's dollars – and must keep paying to get any return.

It would all be very easy to decide which is the best option if we knew when we were going to die. But short of having a reliable crystal ball, that's an unknown.

Your Will can also set out your wishes concerning organ donation, whether for transplant or scientific purposes.

Understanding Wills and Estate Planning

5. Get ahead of the courts

When you pass, you can leave your assets to anyone you want to. There's nothing to say you can't.

On the mirror side of that, the law says people who fit into certain categories – that is, certain close family members (by statutory entitlement) and people who can establish they were dependent on you for support in some way – have a right to challenge your Will.

Also, you *can* leave someone out altogether.

However, leaving a close family member out doesn't prevent that person challenging the Will. And you will find in some cases Wills are quite successfully challenged, while in other cases their claims are unsuccessful. You can just hear them saying, 'I shouldn't have been disinherited, there are reasons why I should have been given part of the estate'.

The reasons for leaving someone out might be: (1) they're independently wealthy, (2) they haven't had much contact with the deceased, and (3) there is no dependency. The courts may conclude, 'Yes, you were left out, but there is no reason you should have been included. You have enough wealth in your own right to not need this money, therefore the deceased should be allowed to leave it to other family members who are more in need than you are'.

On the other hand, if the court forms the view that the person who was left out *does need support*, then they may grant that support, even though the Will has left them out.

The author of a Will can do whatever s/he likes, but the courts have the authority to overrule the Will if it doesn't think the right thing has been done.

This means that the 'black sheep' of the family, who may have been a financial drain on parents for years, can often prove *financial dependency*. This may justify being apportioned a share of the estate despite the parents feeling s/he has already had a fair share via an early inheritance (of sorts).

If you're considering leaving a family member out of your Will, seek advice so that the Will and supporting documents can be prepared in such a way that the chances of a successful challenge is minimised.

Unfortunately, the only constant in this area is that the court's decision in any particular case is largely unpredictable. Other than in obvious cases, even the experts who specialise in this type of litigation have great difficulty in predicting what the courts may decide.

The decision to fight or negotiate a payment is hard for the executor. The cost to an estate of defending a challenge may result in the executors paying a claim (or part of it) simply to avoid the high costs and long delays associated with court proceedings. Again, sound legal advice is critical when faced with a challenge.

NSW/NOTIONAL ESTATE LAW

The laws do vary from state to state, and New South Wales has a law in this area that no other state currently has.

NSW has a concept of 'notional estate'. That is, if I own assets and within three years of dying, I think, 'I want to cut that son out, but he'll challenge the Will, so what I'll do before I die is I'll give assets away to my other two children, so when I die, I've got nothing left'. The child who misses out can apply to the court and assert that s/he should have received a share. If the court says, 'Yes, you should have been given part of the estate' then the court is confronted with a problem. There's nothing in the estate because it was disposed of at a date prior to death.

The courts in NSW have the power to call back those assets and redistribute them as if they remained the property of the deceased at the time of death. Even if someone has had a property registered in their name for the last two years, they could be ordered to return ownership to the estate, so it can be distributed as part of the estate. Assets that have been disposed of in this way can be treated as if they remain assets of the estate and that's why it's referred to as 'notional estate'. In this way, **the courts can claw back assets that a person disposed of,** to satisfy claims that the deceased attempted to avoid. In the future, it's likely that this law will extend to other States.

Even if you live outside NSW, be warned, because if you own assets in NSW this law will catch those assets.

The types of transactions that can be treated as a 'disposal' for clawing back 'notional estate' are surprisingly broad. Even the *failure to exercise options to purchase shares* or failure to *alter the control of a trust* and other obscure transactions can be treated as a disposal for the purposes of this law. So extreme caution must be exercised if a person wants to tread this path.

IF YOU WANT TO CHALLENGE A WILL

People often have quiet genuine reasons and justification for challenging a Will when they haven't been adequately provided for. Each State and Territory has legislation that specifies details concerning;

- Who is eligible to challenge a Will (usually close family members such as a spouse and children and people who were dependant on the deceased)?
- Matters that must be proven to satisfy a court that it should change the terms of the Will.

The complexities of this topic are beyond the scope of this book.

6. The 'x' and the 'black-sheep' factor

Some people make a lot of money at a certain point of their lives, followed by a drop in income as time passes. Sportspeople and models peak at a young age. Pop stars are the same, unless they transform themselves into 'musicians' and/or songwriters. Pickled and preserved they can then last for years.

However, during their most fruitful period, they may have had a partner, and perhaps a different one in their less fruitful times.

If there was no property settlement when they broke up with their first partner, then the first partner's claim to assets within the deceased estate would still survive. S/he might simply say, 'Not only do I have a claim against the estate on the basis that s/he was my ex-partner, but the assets in the estate are partly owned by me anyway – because I was married to/living with this person during the prosperous period and s/he made all this money partly through (or 'because of') my influence and support'.

S/he would run the same argument as if s/he'd launched a Family Law property claim. They might say, 'All the assets in his estate aren't necessarily all his, half are owned by me. They might be in his name but, under the Family Law Act, I'm entitled to half. So, let's take out what I own, and what's left should be the estate'.

PROPERTY CLAIMS BEFORE DEATH

A husband may draft a Will leaving everything to the children of his first marriage. His current wife of 10 years thinks that's unfair so before he dies, while he's suffering dementia, she commences a property law claim under the Family Law Act claiming half his assets. She serves the court application one day before he dies.

What happens?

The Family Law claim proceeds and is heard even if the husband has died. By the time the Family Law matter is finished the deceased estate is likely to only receive half his assets (or some other portion) and thus his wishes are defeated.

FAMILY PROVISIONS

Certain categories of people (spouse and children for example) have the right to challenge a Will if they believe that the deceased failed to make adequate provision for them. This right however isn't limited to close family members; it extends to people who may have been financially dependent on the deceased. The nature and extent of the type of 'dependency' that may get a claimant across the line is broad. Often not always obvious to family and other onlookers. Just being caring toward, or providing financial assistance to, a stranger or 'the black sheep in the family' might even give that stranger/ blacksheep a right to claim.

COTTAGE OCCUPANT

Mary and her husband retired to a hobby farm. Mary's husband, a kind soul, allowed an old war time colleague (who wasn't a friend) down on his luck to live in the tiny workers' cottage on the farm in exchange for helping out as a handy man around the farm.

Her husband died and left his whole estate to Mary. Mary allowed her husband's old colleague to continue to live in the cottage even though by this time he was too frail to do much around the farm. Mary died and left everything to her children.

The cottage occupant challenged her Will claiming she made inadequate provision for him as he was financially dependent on her. He claimed she should have made provision for his future accommodation. He succeeded.

Leaving an adult ('black sheep') child out of your Will because you have financially supported them throughout your life can be fraught with danger. The very fact that you had to keep helping them could well arm the child with a strong argument that s/he was dependant on you.

It's a sad thing that we must be careful about who we are kind to.

DE FACTOS

As a rule of thumb, two years gives a de facto relationship legal credence. It's cumulative, so 12 months, followed by a six-month breakup, followed by another 12 months = two years. The six months spell doesn't count.

But if a child is born at any time during that relationship, that child makes a big difference to that partner's entitlements. A one-night-stand resulting in a child could give birth to an entitlement to a share of the father's estate by the mother and the child. You can basically forget the two-year rule when a child comes along.

Even after as little as six months a claim can be made if it can be argued that the surviving partner is a dependent as a matter of fact. The surviving partner can reason, 'Even though we've only been together a short time, I gave up my work to manage the house, and I became financially dependent on him/her. So, because I was dependent, s/he should have made appropriate provision in the Will to maintain me in the lifestyle to which I became accustomed.'

ADEQUATE PROVISION

When Charlie married Vicki, it was his third marriage, and her second. They jointly contributed to buying a home, which they owned 50/50. In addition to that, over the period of their marriage, they acquired a couple of investment properties in Charlie's name. In their senior years they lived off the rental income from those properties.

In his Will, Charlie gave most of his share of the home to the children of his other marriages as well as dividing the two investment properties amongst his children.

So, although Vicki was left with slightly more than her half share of the property, the Will required her to sell the property which put her in a position where she didn't have enough money to buy a replacement home. She also lost her sources of income – the two investment properties.

So, she challenged the Will on the basis that Charlie didn't make adequate provision for her. The outcome: the court let Vicki keep those properties for the rest of her life. On the basis that the Will did not leave adequate provision for Vicki, the court concluded, 'While you're alive you can continue to have the home and the investment properties for the income, and Charlie's Will can be implemented after you die'.

CHALLENGING A WILL

Generally speaking, the only people who can challenge a Will as of right are family – that is the spouse/s and children of a deceased person. The one area where the specifications of a Will may open up to cover just about anybody is people who claim that they were in part or whole a **dependent**.

SEVERAL TOP 10 HITS LATER

Col was the drummer in a 1970s Rock band that enjoyed several Top 10 hits, and later, cover versions of their songs. Although Col played on the hits, he didn't write them. To keep a balance within the band members' earnings, the singer-songwriter gave Col a small royalty. He didn't have to, but it seemed fair. Col didn't want his mate the 55-year-old drummer living on the streets and this small royalty became Col's staple income. It was okay – they were mates.

*When the singer-songwriter died, his wife didn't feel the same obligation to Col. She decided to stop the payments. This was contested in court, Col reasoned, 'I am actually **dependent** on the money I received from him...' and Col's lawyer reasoned that because* there's an obligation to provide for the people who are dependent on you, the singer-songwriter's Will should have made provision for Col. And he won.

So, even if they're not a family member, if someone can prove they need the money – say – to pay their rent, then they can claim against the estate. And if the court is satisfied that assertion is true, the estate must continue to provide that share of the income, because they need it and the deceased knew they needed it.

7. Take care of beneficiaries with disabilities

(also refer to chapter nine − Testamentary trusts)

Letter to a client with two daughters and a son with a disability (a poor letter at that):

Dear Mr and Ms Jones,

You have instructed me to prepare Wills that leave most of your estate to a trust to care for your disabled son. The monies held in the trust will be distributed equally between your daughters (or their descendants) when your son dies.

I'm sure your daughters are well aware of the needs of their brother and that you wish to plan for how these will be met once you're gone.

I would urge you to *be open and honest with your daughters, advising them of the legal advice you have been given and involve them in the process of drafting and preparing your Will*.

This won't only reduce any likelihood of shock and disappointment, but it will also give you the opportunity to convey in person what you're hoping to achieve and work through any disharmony.

If it's too distressing for you to talk to your daughters directly, or you're confused by the legal language used, then I'm happy to explain everything to them. Sometimes *a third party* can remove the confusion and emotion often felt when talking about death and dying, particularly where your daughters may view their brother's interest in your estate as unfairly competing with their own.

I encourage you to deal with this potentially contentious issue while you're alive rather than leaving disappointment and potential conflict as your legacy to your children.

I wish you luck and look forward to hearing back from you.

Sincerely

Rod Cunich TEP
Estate Planning and Wealth Protection Lawyer

Alternate letter to same client (a more thoughtful/professional version):

Dear Mr and Ms Jones,

You have instructed me to prepare Wills that leave most of your estate to a trust to care for your disabled son. The monies held in the trust will be distributed equally between your daughters (or their descendants) when your son dies.

I confirm my advice in conference that before proceeding I recommend that you engage the services of a financial planner to help you determine exactly how much needs to be set aside for your son taking into account his disability pension and his Centrelink benefits.

Leaving him too much money may work to his disadvantage as it may adversely affect his benefits.

Further, I recommended that you contact Centrelink's SDT Assessment team and have your son assessed to see if he qualifies for the benefits of a special disability trust. If he does then there are estate-planning options that can be used to maximise accommodation, care and lifestyle benefits for your son without adversely affecting his Centrelink benefits.

Not only will these steps ensure you adopt the best approach for your son, but it may result in much less having to be set aside for your son and thus available to your daughters when you pass away.

I would urge you to *be open and honest with your daughters, advising them of the legal advice you have been given and involve them in the estate planning process.*

I wish you luck and look forward to hearing back from you.

Sincerely

Rod Cunich TEP
Estate Planning and Wealth Protection Lawyer

There are numerous *legal structures* that can be utilised to address the situation of a beneficiary with a disability. To succeed, this structure must be coordinated with your financial planning and retirement plans.

It's all up to you. The beneficiary has a disability, remember? And might be unable to defend his/her rights, on his/her own behalf. You have the responsibility to inform yourself.

First: consult with your other children and make an assessment of their respective financial positions.

Next: consult a specialist financial planner to help you undertake some disability tailored financial modelling.

This process will help you work out accurately:
- How much money will be available when you die,
- How much will be required to support your child – balancing, Centrelink benefits, the cost of accommodation and a multitude of similar practical considerations,
- What will be available to your other children on (1) your death, and (2) on the subsequent death of your disabled child, and,
- Funding options to achieve your desired outcomes including the use of life insurance, annuities, superannuation and funds management.

This type of modelling will help identify what legal options are most appropriate to your circumstances, and what 'fairness' might look like in reality.

ADVICE

I recommend that a financial adviser who specialises in this type of modelling be engaged hand-in-hand with your lawyer to work out the optimum solution for your circumstances.

I recommend that you have your child assessed by Centrelink to determine whether s/he qualifies for a Special Disability Trust.

Some of the legal structures commonly used in combination with this type of financial advice are:

1. A **Special Disability Trust** created while you're alive or written into your Will. This type of trust can be used to assist with the provision of care and accommodation without impacting on Centrelink benefits. These trusts are restricted to severely disabled people, so you would best have your child assessed by Centrelink to determine if s/he does qualify. Only a small part of the trust fund can be used for lifestyle and other uses — provision of care and accommodation are the focus of this type of trust.

2. An **All Needs Protective Trust** created while you're alive or written into your Will. These trusts are much more flexible than Special Disability Trusts as the funds can be used for all purposes including lifestyle needs, such as holidays and hobbies. And there is no restriction on who can use them. The shortcoming however, is that income generated by property owned by the trust and capital in the trust will count towards the Centrelink Means Tests (so care must be taken not to adversely affect Centrelink benefits).

3. A **combination** of both types of trust.

Your other children can be involved in the management of the trusts as trustees or 'family advisors'.

If your disabled child passes away before their siblings the remaining capital in both these trusts can revert back to your other children, or their descendants.

PROVIDING CERTAINTY FOR FAMILIES WHO HAVE A CHILD WITH A DISABILITY

What is my current pet project?

Let me set the scene for you. Parents of children with a disability find it hard to plan for their child's long-term future: who'll care for their child when they can't, where will they live, will there be sufficient money for their care – how much is enough?

For many parents, their future is limited to *getting through their day*.

Rarely do these parents have the time, or head space, to think about their own future. Issues such as financial planning for their own retirement or the basic preparation of a Will and other essential succession planning needs don't see the light of day. Even the concept of retirement seems too remote to contemplate at all.

With no starting point to begin with, no end game they can identify and no milestones to measure progress along the way, it's simply been too hard. These families rank amongst those most in need of certainty and clarity around their family's future but must live with a future clouded by uncertainty.

There is now some hope.
In recent years I have been collaborating with
• an experienced service provider that undertakes a costed, lifetime care needs analysis for disabled persons, and

- a reputable investment planning organisation to develop an innovative, integrated planning service to help these families.

This service is the first of its kind in Australia, perhaps in the world. In four steps we now give parents the ability to
- identify and cost with clarity, of a disabled child's lifetime needs,
- identify and cost of the parents own life time needs,
- then build a comprehensive financial and succession plan that provides for the parent's future and the integrated support for their child's long-term care even after they pass away, and
- ongoing reviews to adjust for the unforeseen.

It is a new way of approaching families who have a child with disabilities. It creates financial certainty and a safe and fulfilling life plan for their future and their child's future.

Like every successful plan, the first important step is knowledge. Through one on one interviews in the home environment, occupational therapists prepare an assessment and support plan for the child's current and future needs. This gives us a thorough understanding of the parent's and child's aspirations and the reasonable and necessary support they require to lead a fulfilling life – whilst the parents are alive and below that time.

Secondly, with the help and involvement of financial planners we provide a costed budget for the services required to fulfil the assessment and support plan, determining the funds required to deliver the services the child needs both now and into the future.
Through a scenario modelling presentation and a comprehensive financial plan together we can evaluate the family's current financial position, integrating current situations with desired future outcomes and develop a plan to achieve those goals. For the parents,

the disabled child, and other children. Visual demonstrations of scenarios are used to help parents make choices along the way.

Once these goals are set and the plan made, your estate planning professional completes phase three, providing specialist estate planning legal advice and documentation to underpin the families' plans. All the potential legal ramifications are considered while Wills, Enduring Powers of Attorney and other Family Agreements are individually tailored to include all elements of the agreed plan.

The final, and essential fourth step is the plan's implementation and ongoing review, ensuring consistent quality control to best support the child's needs, for today and tomorrow.

In one process and from one collaborative team we have ensured that the right decisions are made at the right time for children with disabilities. A full, integrated assessment and support plan is created with the knowledge we need to understand each family and child's current and future requirements.

The financial provisions of that plan are evaluated, with steps to achieve the required financial outcomes to facilitate those provisions.

Essential legal safeguards are completed to ensure that the plan allies with legal issues, with no complicated future concerns.

And the plan is fully executed and managed with superior quality control measures, for the betterment of each child's future.
It is fair to say that this is an innovative approach to support planning. Not only does it represent the future of the families and disabled children, but in some capacity, it represents the future of the disability support planning industry.

8. Probate and estate administration

Probate involves an application to the courts to formally approve your Will and authorise your executor to act in accordance with the terms of the Will.

The courts issue a *Grant of Probate* that looks like a certificate. Executors can produce the Grant of Probate to satisfy others that they have the power to act under the Will. Sighting the Grant of Probate is often a pre-condition that banks, the Land Titles Office and the Share Registry require before they will transfer assets on the instructions of an executor.

The cost of obtaining a Grant of Probate depends on the value of the assets in the estate. It varies in each state from as little as $1000 to about $5000. It can be more than that if it's a wealthy estate. There is a scale in each state that's used to determine the cost however you can contract out of this scale in most states – not NSW.

EXECUTOR

An executor is the person appointed by a will to act on the behalf of the estate of the testator ('will maker') on his or her death. An executor is the legal personal representative of a deceased person's estate. Appointment of an executor only becomes effective after the death of the will maker. An executor can decline to act when the will maker dies as there is no legal obligation for that person to accept the appointment.

An executor has very broad powers to deal with the deceased's assets and to wind up their affairs.

ADMINISTRATOR

When a person dies without a Will then the legal personal representative who plays the role of an executor is known as an 'Administrator' who is appointed by the court at the request of an interest party – often a beneficiary. Administrators are commonly a close relative, but not necessarily.

THE PROBATE PROCESS

In Australia, there is a Supreme Court probate registry in each State and Territory that deals with probate applications. Each however has slightly different laws and processes in relation to probate. The main probate legislation is as follows:
- In New South Wales, the Probate and Administration Act 1898 (NSW).
- In Victoria, the Administration and Probate Act 1958 (VIC).
- In Queensland, the Uniform Civil Procedure Rules 1999.
- In Western Australia, the Non-contentious Probate Rules 1967 (WA).
- In South Australia, the Administration and Probate Act 1919 (SA).
- In Tasmania, the Administration and Probate Act 1935 (TAS).
- In the ACT, the Administration and Probate Act 1929 (ACT).
- In the Northern Territory, the Administration and Probate Act 1993 (NT).

In very general terms the process looks a bit like this:
- The executor must file in court an application for probate together with the affidavit evidence required by the local legislation. The evidence includes details of assets and a copy of the Will.

- Legal notices must be published to put creditors and all other interested parties on notice of the application – including persons who may wish to challenge the will.
- Once probate is granted, the executor must gather in, secure and protect the assets and after payment of all expenses and debts (including tax) and then must distribute assets in accordance with the terms of the Will. Sometimes real estate or other property may need to be sold to facilitate the distribution of assets pursuant to the Will or merely to pay debts.
- Executor usually seeks legal and accounting guidance in how to administer the deceased estate, how to take creditors' rights into account and when to distribute assets
- There are strict time frames involved in filing and objecting to claims against the estate.
- Costs of the administration including ordinary taxation such as income tax on interest and property taxation is deducted from assets in the estate before distribution by the executors of the will.
- Other assets may simply need to be transferred from the deceased to his or her beneficiaries. Other assets may have pay on death or transfer on death designations, which avoids probate, such as life insurance and superannuation death benefits.
- The rights of beneficiaries must be respected. They must be given proper and adequate notice, distribution of estate assets must be timely and the executor must otherwise administer the estate properly and efficiently.

The administration of a deceased estate (timing and cost) varies according to the value and complexity of the estate. If the value of the estate is relatively small, then it might be possible to avoid the probate process. In some jurisdictions and/or at a certain value threshold, probate must be applied for by the executor or administrator.

CHANGING RULES

The laws regulating Wills and estate administration are in the process of evolving. Governments are trying to introduce uniform laws across all states and territories.

We aren't there yet (by a long shot unfortunately), so it remains a bit of a lucky dip as to how your Will or your estate will be dealt with, depending on where you live and where your assets are located.

As outlined in chapter one, one example is the **intestacy laws**. In some states if you die without a will everything goes to a surviving partner whilst in other states the estate is split up between spouse and children. Add to the mix an ex-spouse, a current de facto and children from both (or a third relationship!) and the outcomes can vary beyond belief between states.

In NSW, a wife can find herself sharing an estate with a mistress and her children and having to negotiate a 'deal' with them. Preparing a Will and keeping it current is the only way you can ensure certainty. At least then if a third party launches a claim against the estate challenging the Will the surviving spouse has a known position to defend, it's not all up for grabs.

9. Testamentary trusts

Before you begin reading this chapter, take a deep breath. It deals with one of the more complex types of Will, but understanding the options offered is well worth the effort, even if you decide testamentary trusts aren't for you. An informed decision to reject is better than an ill-informed decision to accept or reject.

What is a testamentary trust?

They are simply a <u>trust</u> created by a Will into which money or other assets are transferred from a deceased estate. The trust receives the inheritance rather than the individual beneficiary. The trust comes into effect after the Willmaker's death.

They can take many forms, but the most common version is where money or other assets are left to a trust where the trustee can make discretionary distributions to the spouse, children, grandchildren and other relatives of the Willmaker. In many respects, these discretionary testamentary trusts are like **family trusts**. The underlying beneficiary controls the trust as trustee and can manage his/her inheritance almost as if it had been received personally, but the trust provides asset protection and tax benefits not available if the gift has been received personally by the beneficiaries.

In broad terms testamentary trusts can be explained in a diagram such as this:

If everything is to be left to a **single beneficiary:**

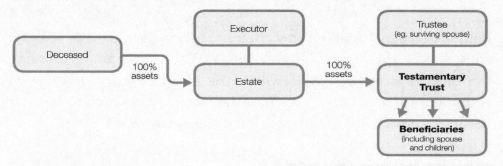

If there is **more than one beneficiary**, for example the division of your estate between children:

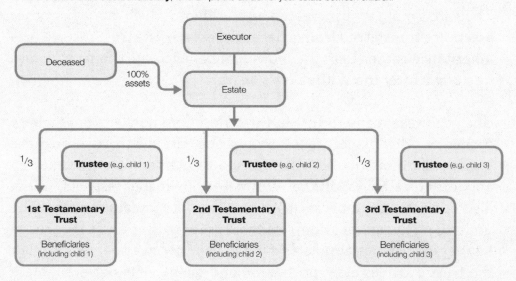

When should you consider using a testamentary trust?

They are particularly useful if:
- you have a substantial estate and you want to distribute it in a tax effective manner;
- you wish to provide beneficiaries with an asset protection structure they can use to fend off treats to their inheritance such as creditors in the event of financial failure or a spouse/partner in the event of relationship breakdown;
- you want to set aside money to provide for the education and upbringing of your children or grandchildren;
- you want to leave a gift to a beneficiary who's intellectually challenged or who can't look after their own affairs and you want someone else manage the gift for them; or
- you want to leave a gift to a beneficiary who has financial problems (e.g. a bankrupt, spendthrift or someone suffering a drug or gambling problem) and you want someone else to manage it for them so that they don't waste it.

What are the advantages of a testamentary trust?

One of the major advantages of testamentary trusts is how income distributed to children is taxed. Ordinarily, if someone under 18 receives 'unearned income' (such as distributions from a family trust), they're subject to a small tax-free threshold and will pay high rates of tax (up to 66% on some portions of the income) above that level.

However, income received by someone under 18 from a testamentary trust is subject to the normal adult tax-free threshold (currently $18,200) and normal adult marginal tax rates above that level. This effectively allows minors to currently receive up to $18,200 per annum tax free (these amounts change from time to time).

ASSET PROTECTION

Testamentary trusts also offer asset protection and special provision for looking after beneficiaries with special needs, such as those who are intellectually challenged, bankrupt, spendthrift or have issues with drugs or gambling.

There are some disadvantages however.

The disadvantages of a testamentary trust?

The main disadvantage is the administration involved, both in terms of time and cost. A testamentary trust might last for many years. The trustee will have to keep proper accounts for the trust and file tax returns every year. The costs of doing this eat into the tax savings that can be achieved.

Also, Wills with testamentary trusts are usually more complex and costly to prepare than standard Wills.

For these reasons, a testamentary trust isn't for everyone.

How does a testamentary trust save tax?

If:
- your estate includes a substantial sum of money or income producing investments;
- in the ordinary course, you would leave your estate to an adult beneficiary (say, your spouse/partner, a sibling or an adult child) who has children under 18; and
- there is a reasonable possibility of that beneficiary investing the gift they receive to earn income rather than spending it on non-income producing assets – such as a house to live in,

then you should strongly consider including a discretionary testamentary trust in your Will. Substantial tax savings can be achieved. Depending your circumstances, the overall tax payable on the income earned by the trust and distributed for the benefit of children is likely to be substantially less than the tax that would be payable by the adult beneficiary if they were to earn that income in their own name.

SO, LET ME GIVE YOU AN EXAMPLE

The tax rates change from time to time. This example is based on tax rates at the time of drafting.

Mary wants to leave her estate to her husband Tom. He currently pays the top marginal tax rate (including Medicare levy) of 47%. Mary and Tom have two minor children who attend private schools and don't earn any income. Assume that on her death Mary's estate, if invested, would generate income of $40,000 per year.

Scenario I

If Mary left her estate to Tom outright (i.e. not in a discretionary testamentary trust) and he received the $40,000 income per year, then his after-tax position would be:

	Tom
Income	$40,000
Tax + Medicare levy	$18,800
Low income tax offset (only applicable where taxable income is less than $66,667)	nil
Net Income after tax	$21,200

If the income was divided equally between Mary and Tom's children (either via an existing family trust or an outright gift), the after-tax position of the children would be:

	Child A	Child B	Combined
Income	$20,000	$20,000	$40,000
Tax[14]	$9,000	$9,000	$18,000
Net Income after tax	$11,000	$11,000	$22,000

You can see that because they're minors they effectively pay a penalty tax, making distribution to minors very unattractive.

Scenario 2

If instead Mary leaves her estate to a discretionary testamentary trust with Tom as the trustee and the trust income is distributed equally between Mary and Tom's children, the after-tax position would be:

	Child A	Child B	Combined
Income	$20,000	$20,000	$40,000
Tax[16]	nil	nil	nil
Net receipt	$20,000	$20,000	$40,000

Using a testamentary trust delivers a much better tax outcome than either of the options in scenario 1. There is a substantial tax saving and Mary and Tom can use the money to pay their children's school fees and other living expenses.

SUMMARY OF BENEFIT

In this example, the discretionary testamentary trust saves **$18,800** tax per annum, leaving more available to spend on the children's education and welfare. The tax savings that can be achieved by using a testamentary trust will depend on the individual circumstances of the Willmaker and their family members. In particular, it will depend on the tax position of their adult beneficiaries, how many children under 18 those beneficiaries have and the tax position of those children.

An accountant or tax adviser will be able to advise you about the tax benefits of a testamentary trust in your circumstances.

I want to set up a fund for the benefit of an infant. How should I best do this?

You can achieve this quite simply by making a gift to the infant and then relying on:

- The legal position that a gift to a person under 18 won't vest in them until they turn 18 (or any later <u>vesting age</u> you may specify in your Will); and
- The provision in most standard Wills allowing an executor to 'advance' the gift for the education, welfare or benefit of an infant beneficiary.

This involves placing a fair degree of trust in your executor – for example, that they'll continue to hold the gift in trust for the infant and they'll also exercise their power to 'advance' the gift in a manner consistent with your wishes. They also need to invest the moneys wisely. It's a big task.

Alternatively, you could set up a more formal testamentary trust specifying how you want the gift dealt with. These types of more formal testamentary trusts need to be carefully structured to ensure that they meet your objectives and cater for your family's individual circumstances.

I want to leave a gift to someone who is mentally incapacitated or who can't look after their own affairs. How should I best do this?

The best way to do this would be to set up a testamentary trust. The executor or another nominated trustee would hold the gift on trust for the beneficiary and apply any income received and perhaps even some of the capital for their benefit (e.g. paying their living or medical expenses).

These types of testamentary trusts need to be carefully structured to ensure that they meet your objectives and cater for your child's circumstances without adversely affecting their Centrelink entitlements (refer to chapter seven).

I want to leave a gift to someone who has problems looking after money and I want to make sure that they don't squander it. How should I best do this?

The best way to do this would be to set up a testamentary trust. The executor or another trustee would hold the gift on trust for the beneficiary in question and make payments to the beneficiary in their discretion or as you direct in your Will.

If you're concerned that the beneficiary might become bankrupt and don't want the money or investments you leave them used to pay off their creditors, you can also set up a so-called 'protective trust', where the beneficiary's interest in the trust terminates upon their bankruptcy.

These types of testamentary and protective trusts need to be carefully structured to ensure that they meet your objectives and cater for your family's individual circumstances.

10. Death and taxes

An often-cited quote is that of Benjamin Franklin who stated... *'In this world nothing can be said to be certain, except death and taxes'*. It can be frustrating to see to the lengths that some people will go to, to manage their tax affairs throughout their life to only then fail to identify that upon their respective death these two events can often unintentionally collide without some careful tax planning.

It is for this reason, I've added two chapters that discuss from a basic level, the taxation implications and considerations of death. These chapters were originally prepared for me by my good friend, Ian Raspin[17] for which I am most grateful, and I've made a few modifications to fit the style of this book[18].

This chapter looks at some of the tax issues that you should consider as part of your estate planning process. It will assist your executor in administering your estate, and importantly identify how you might preserve the balance of your estate for your beneficiaries by saving considerable, and often avoidable, taxation and administration costs.

When it comes to your tax affairs, the Income Tax Assessment Act squarely places the executor of your estate straight into your shoes. They have the same tax responsibilities and obligations over your affairs as you have prior to your death. Your executor will have full access to all your assets to meet your tax obligations, and more importantly, they will also be personal liability to the ATO if they fail to pay your taxes, thus placing their own personal assets at risk. Who'd be an executor you might ask.

It is important therefore that you consider the tax related issues and information that you are passing on to your executor to ensure they can meet their obligations.

PRIOR YEAR INCOME TAX RETURNS

If you have outstanding personal Income Tax Returns when you pass away, it will be your executor's responsibility to address each and every outstanding Tax Return.

At face value, this may not sound too bad. But let's step into an executor's shoes and have another look.

Imagine your neighbour appoints you their executor and on their passing you are now faced with the obligation to prepare and lodge the last two years of Income Tax Returns for them and be personally liable for any unpaid tax if you get it wrong.

You'd be confronted with the prospect of finding out what income they had, whether they had properties, what if any shares do they held, what deductions they are entitled to, what about superannuation caps or contributions apply? Lots to consider. Most of it a mystery to you.

To make it even harder, how do you now identify and locate all the documentation to capture and substantiate everything that you are going to have to declare as accurate in their outstanding Income Tax Returns?

Ian tells me that the worst situation he's experienced is 33 years of outstanding Returns! It resulted in a near seven figure tax liability, not to mention associated interest and penalties, and naturally substantial stress and hair loss for a frustrated Executor.

Don't do that to your executor.

To assist your executor, keep a copy of your last year's Tax Return, Tax File Number and the accumulation of this year's documentation in one safe and secure location for easy access.

CAPITAL AND INCOME LOSSES

If you have either prior year capital or income losses being carried forward in your personal Income Tax Return, it is important to understand that these **losses do not transfer across** to your Estate and that the future tax benefits of these losses are ordinarily lost upon death. Your Estate is treated as a separate legal taxpayer to yourself, and just as I cannot transfer any tax losses that I may have to you, you are equally unable to transfer losses across to your Estate.

For clarity, capital losses are those losses created upon the sale of assets such as shares, while income losses for example are created by conducting a property that are running at a loss. Capital losses can only be absorbed by capital gains, while income losses can generally (with exceptions) be used to absorb both capital gains and other income.

If you have carried forward capital losses in your Tax Returns, it may be worth considering discussing these with your financial advisor. If you die before using these losses, they will be lost to your beneficiaries. They'll have to pay tax on the unrealised capital gains they inherit from you **when and if they physically sell the inherited assets**. Subject to advice, it's sometimes better to sell assets while you are alive, so your capital gains can be offset against your capital losses thereby maximising the return from the sale.

There is of courses an exception: if you plan to transfer a capital asset to an overseas beneficiary or charity (which isn't a Deductible Gift Recipient) there is a deemed disposal for Capital Gains Tax purposes that will occur on your death and must be declared by the executor in your final personal Income Tax Return. Where this occurs, any carried forward capital losses held in your name could be utilised at this point.

HISTORY OF ASSETS

One of the surest methods to deplete your estate is to not have left critical details about when and for how much you acquired certain assets, particularly share portfolios.

Your executor is going to need this information, no matter if they are selling your assets and distributing cash, and need to calculate how much Capital Gains Tax they need to pay, or if you have instructed them to transfer the asset to your beneficiary(s), to meet their obligations in providing your beneficiaries with their inherited cost base information.

Many thousands of dollars in fees can quickly accumulate as executors try to either reconstruct cost bases. With dividend reinvestment programs, demergers and share splits they task can be difficult and time consuming. These costs can be easily avoided by maintaining adequate records to pass on to your executor.

It is equally as important to retain this sort of information about assets that you may have inherited during your own lifetime as several factors can impact the deemed or inherited costs bases you may have received and are now transferring to your own beneficiaries.

OFFSHORE ASSETS

In June 2016, the Australian Bureau of Statistics reported that 28.5% of Australia's estimated population (6.9 million people) were born overseas. With such a high immigration rate and ever-growing global economy, it is understandable why so many Australians hold assets abroad.

While it is important to ensure these assets are dealt with adequately in your estate plan, it is equally important to appreciate that the Australian tax system imposes income tax on the global assets and the income of all Australian tax residents.

Remember, your executor is personally responsible to address your outstanding income tax affairs, which would extend to them obtaining knowledge of any non-reported income and assets that you may have held abroad. Executors often wish to bring the assets or their cash equivalent back into Australia for the beneficiaries, to either pay off their own mortgage or improve their lives here. They are then faced with a retrospective tax compliance issue, personal executorial liability and the fact that the transfer of funds into Australia will be tracked by Federal regulators.

Having seen executors navigate these painful waters, if you have any such issues, its strongly recommend that you seek specialist tax advice and addressing them head on as part of your estate planning issues − this is an area that Ian can help. I have seen many, once grateful beneficiaries, turn resentful because they are left to manage this type of legacy issues

On the other hand, if your affairs are in order, then it is more critical than ever in relation to your Australian based assets, to ensure you record cost base information for your offshore interests. It can be significantly more difficult for an Executor to obtain these details from some overseas jurisdictions.

Understanding Wills and Estate Planning

II. Your estate and taxes

How a deceased estate is taxed. Knowing the answer may be of relevance to you if you are going to act as an executor for someone else, or to assist in understanding the process your own affairs will go through when you pass away.

Like the last chapter, the original draft of this chapter was prepared by Ian Raspin[19].

Although Australia abolished a direct Death Tax in 1978 we do have several indirect taxes and taxation trigger points that arise because of death which can create several complexities.

TAX STATUS

When a taxpayer passes away, their taxation status as an Australian taxpayer is also considered to have ceased to have exist. This raises several issues:

1. A final Tax Return known as a Date of Death Return, may be required to be submitted for the period from 1 July of the relevant year to the date of their passing.

2. The Estate will be treated as an entirely separate legal taxpayer, and if required to lodge Tax Returns, will need to apply for its own Tax File Number.

3. An Estate will be treated as either a resident or a non-resident taxpayer based on where the central management and control

of the estate lies. This will be determined by the tax residency status of your chosen executor. The applicable tax rates and treatment of non-resident taxpayers can significantly differ to resident taxpayers.

TAX RATES

The Australian Income Tax system is comparatively very generous when it comes to how it treats the taxation of Deceased Estates.

With the deceased's final Tax Return, standard adult marginal tax rates will continue to apply, and generously, the tax-free threshold of $18,200 is not proportionally allocated, but will rather apply in full no matter how many days in a financial year the deceased lived. For the first three years of an estate's administration, the Commissioner permits an estate to be taxed at the same marginal rates that apply to standard adult taxpayers, including the $18,200 tax free threshold. This essentially means in the year of death; the deceased and their estate will have a combined tax-free threshold of $36,400. The applicable rates for the 2017 financial year are as detailed below:

FIRST THREE YEARS OF ESTATE ADMINISTRATION

Taxable Income	Tax Payable
0 - $18,200	Nil
$18,201 - $37,000	19% of excess over $18,200
$37,001 - $87,000	$3,572 + 32.5% of excess over $37,000
$87,001 - $180,000	$19,822 + 37% of excess over $87,000
$180,001 and over	$54,232 + 45% of excess over $180,000

In the fourth and subsequent years of Estate administration, concessional marginal tax rates will still apply, however essentially without the $18,200 tax free threshold. For the 2017 financial year these rates are as detailed below:

FOURTH AND SUBSEQUENT YEARS OF ESTATE ADMINISTRATION

Taxable Income	Tax Payable
0 - $416	Nil
$417 - $670	50% of excess over $416
$670 - $37,000	Entire amount from 0 taxed at 19%
$37,001 - $87,000	$7,030 + 32.5% for excess over $37,000
$87,001 - $180,000	$23,280 + 37% of excess over $87,000
$180,001 and over	$57,690 + 45% of excess over $180,000

Note: These rates only apply at the Commissioner's discretion. If he believes an estate administration is being unduly delayed; for example, to take advantage of lower marginal tax rates to those available to beneficiaries, the ATO can apply the highest marginal tax rate to every single dollar of income earned. Currently this penalty rate is 47%.

TRANSFER OF ASSETS

The Income Tax Assessment Act provides rollover relief of assets on death, meaning that in most of cases the transfer of assets on death to either an executor or beneficiary does not trigger a Capital Gains Tax (CGT) event. This effectively defers the unrealised gain or loss on the asset until they are subsequently physically disposed of by either the executor or the beneficiary. In other words, a beneficiary inherits the asset with an existing debt associated with it (the capital gains liability) which must be paid when the beneficiary eventually sells the property.

Still with me? If so, here are a few points to note:

* A disposal of an asset during the administration of the estate will trigger a CGT event within the estate.
* The executor would ordinarily pay the Capital Gains Tax on an asset disposed of during the estate administration.
* The beneficiary will pay Capital Gains Tax on an asset they inherited when they subsequently dispose of the asset after receipt.

INHERITED COST BASE OF ASSETS

There are some special 'deemed acquisition' rules for Capital Gains Tax purposes.

* For assets purchased by the deceased prior to 20 September 1985 (pre-CGT), they are deemed to have a market value at date of death, and a date of acquisition at date of death. That is, they become subject to CGT on and from death. They are no longer CGT exempt.
* For assets purchased on or after 20 September 1985, the assets are deemed to be acquired by the beneficiary at the deceased's cost base, and at date of death.

However, if the asset is sold less than 12 months after date of death, the 50% CGT discount is still available for post-CGT assets as the deceased's acquisition date is considered during the calculations.

PRINCIPAL PLACE OF RESIDENCE

Most people know that the sale of their principal place of residence is generally exempt from Capital Gains Tax. This concept is extended to a deceased estate in that the legislation permits the sale of a deceased persons' residence to also be exempt from Capital Gains Tax, where the executor **both sells and settles the sale of the property within two years of date of death.**

The exemption can also be extended when it becomes the principal place of residence of the deceased's spouse/partner, or an individual with a right to occupy under the terms of a Will, or a beneficiary to who uses it as their principal place of residence.

The taxation complexities relating to a deceased's residence can however be a total minefield, with several traps and related issues relating to the use of the property, dates of acquisitions, how the property was held, capital improvements and even tax residency of the deceased, the executor and/or beneficiaries. These complexities are too detailed for this book but are set out in a dedicated book by Ian Raspin entitled '*CGT on a Deceased's Residence, a tax minefield*'.

SUPERANNUATION DEATH BENEFITS

Superannuation is usually one of the largest assets of a typical deceased estate. On the death of a member the Superannuation Fund must payout the member's entitlements (death benefits) as soon as practicable after death. Death benefits attract various tax consequences.

In determining who payments are to be paid to the Superannuation Fund must ensure the payments are permitted by both the Trust Deed and Superannuation law.

If permitted by the Deed, a member of the Fund may have elected to provide the Trustee with specific instructions in advance of their death via either a Binding Death Benefit Nomination (BDBN) or through the establishment of what is known as a Reversionary Pension, which is essentially the continuance payment of a deceased's pension to their spouse. In the absence of such instructions, there may be a substantial delay in paying out superannuation proceeds as the Trustee works through the complexities of determining who a payment is to be made to.

Superannuation can either be paid out as an ongoing income stream directly to beneficiaries, or as a lump sum payment paid directly to either the beneficiaries or to the member's estate. Importantly it is only when the payment is made to the estate that superannuation as such is considered an estate asset.

There is a growing trend of Superannuation Funds opting to pay death benefits to the deceased member's estate, as this transfers the responsibility for considering the taxation consequences from the Superannuation Fund to the executor of the estate.

Where an estate receives a Superannuation Death Benefit Payment, tax will be levied on this payment based on the applicable rate payable had it been paid directly to the ultimate beneficiary. Importantly, where payments are to be paid to either a dependent or interdependent of the deceased, these payments will be considered as tax free, whereas payments to a non-dependent (including most adult children) will be taxable and taxed accordingly against the executor.

The definitional lines between a 'dependent' and a 'non-dependent' can be extremely blurred and hence the tendency to transfer the tax responsibility to the Executor. Again, professional advice should be sought to assist in this process.

It is not possible to detail the complexities of all estate taxation issues in a single chapter, so this chapter is provided only as a high-level overview of some estate matters. It is strongly recommended that professional tax advice be obtained during estate administration, however a small word of caution; this area of tax is not well understood by many practitioners and care should be taken in ensuring you are obtaining an opinion from a suitably experienced practitioner.

12. Your business and estate planning

If you own a business or an interest in a business have you thought about what will happen to it when you retire, become incapacitated or die (business succession planning)?

Your personal estate planning and your business succession planning form part of a single larger picture. They need to be co-ordinated and integrated.

Why?

Answer: Your equity in a business is an asset that one day you will need to convert to cash or arrange to hand over to the next generation. It's critical to your personal estate plan that you plan the future realisation or transfer of your business interest and the transfer of management of your business before it's too late.

How can it ever be too late? According to PwC 69% of business owners currently plan to sell or pass on their business over the next 10 years. Thirty-eight per cent will pass control to the next generation. But 83% don't have a succession plan in place[20].

So, what are the consequences of not having an exit strategy for the equity in a business? It's no secret. The following consequences occur with consistent regularity where the owners haven't planned their exit:

1. Exit occurs due to circumstances that are beyond the owner's control (sickness, accident, loss of mental capacity, death, financial crisis) rather than in accordance with the owner's plans and desire
2. The timetable for exit is forced on the owner due to the circumstances surrounding exit
3. The owner loses control over the process and is left with limited options
4. The owner pays excessive tax
5. The owner ends up selling at an undervalue
6. The owner and their family, and often their staff, suffer high levels of stress
7. The business itself suffers due to poor business continuity
8. Handover to next generation is likely to fail. Only 5% of businesses survive to a 4th generation
9. The owner is not able to achieve their business goals or their personal goals, including their personal estate planning goals

So why do so few business owners plan their exit in advance (remember less than 30% have a plan)? It's often that taking the first step can be the hardest part of the whole process and there are well known barriers that get in the way of tackling that first step:

a) Owners are unsure **how to start** the process or who to approach for help
b) Owners have **difficulty discussing** financial matters and personal goals with others because it is too private, somehow unpleasant, or considered taboo
c) Owners spend all their time **'putting out fires'** and do not have the time to focus on long term planning
d) Owners believe the **time** is **not right** to start the process
e) Owners see the entire process as too **daunting**

f) Owners are afraid of what life without their business would be like. Retirement creates a daunting unspoken fear in the minds of business owners – what if retirement isn't as stimulating or satisfying as running their own business (and like thoughts) and so, they do nothing.

The issues listed above are sometimes referred to as the *'soft issues'* associated with business succession planning. That is, the personal and emotional issues that need to be addressed before the *'hard issues'* (involving financials, taxation, business plans, valuations, management succession, agreements, etc) can be confronted. The soft issues often go unidentified or are consciously ignored because they are too difficult to address and thus the business owner never gets around to dealing with the hard issues involved in preparing their business for sale or handover to the next generation. The soft issues are a major barrier to progress.

Helping business owners identify and understand the soft issues is the first step in the planning process. Helping them create and implement a plan that ensures their retirement will be as personally fulfilling as their business life is what is often necessary to kick start the business succession planning process. The first step.

It is here that experienced professional input can be of great assistance. The first step often involves a few soul-searching heart-to-heart chats and a number of reality checks, followed by structured discussions with business partners and family. There is no set formula. Even though the issues are common, the solutions aren't as every business owner has their own unique set of guiding principles, wishes and concerns. The initial challenge is to identify those principles, wishes and concerns so they can be accommodated.

Once the business owner's personal barriers (the soft issue barriers) to planning are dealt with professionals can then help the business owner deal with the 'hard issues' which require succession planning, including a plan that addresses;

1. Maintenance of key staff through transfer of control and/or equity
2. Long-term business strategy development
3. Determination of value
4. Grooming of management successors
5. Professionalising management and corporate governance
6. Finance and entity structure options
7. Shareholder agreements
8. Developing tax-effective transfer techniques

The planning process can involve various professionals along the way: an accountant, a tax advisor, a valuer, a lawyer, a financial planner and perhaps a business consultant. Some accountants have the skills to address a number of these disciplines (e.g. financial issues, valuation and taxation). Regardless how many are involved, it is important that the professionals work together. Business succession planning is one area where collaboration and team work are critical.

Once a plan is developed it will help the business owner achieve;
- Stress reduction
- Continuity of their business
- Control over when exit occurs
- Control over how exit occurs
- Maximisation of business value
- Minimisation of tax, and
- Achieving business, personal and financial goals

I recently met Tom and Bill who were 78 years of age and had been running an engineering business together since they we in their thirties. Their company employed 135 staff and they were the only shareholders. I asked them the following questions:

- Have you considered retirement?
  Answer: 'no, we enjoy our work.'
- What would happen to the business when one of you does retire, become incapacitated or die?
  Answer: 'haven't thought about it.'
- What is the business worth?
  Answer: 'no idea.'
- Are you each prepared to buy the other's 50% interest of the business if something happens to the other?
  Answer: 'no.'
- Who will run the business when you aren't around?
  Answer: 'there isn't anyone really as we negotiate the contracts and oversee the projects.'
- Have you ever considered selling the business?
  Answer: 'No.'

I was asked to consult with William who imported and distributed a range of small promotional gifts purchased by businesses as giveaways. It was very profitable as the cost of manufacture was low, overheads low and the profit margin high. He'd been unsuccessfully trying to sell for years without success despite many potential buyers enquiring due to the high profits. I asked him a series of questions: who designs the products, do you have contracts with the manufacturers, do you have contracts with your customers, who can run the business in your absence? It transpires the whole enterprise *was completely dependent on William. Although he had staff he controlled everything and there were no formal agreements in place. He simply didn't have a business to sell as no one could 'take it over' with any certainty that the business would continue. My advice: document all relationships and train staff to replace each function you perform. When you can go on holidays for three months without anyone needing to call you, then you have something to sell. It took him five years. He did it.*

In closing, having alerted you to;

- the need for a business succession plan,
- some of the barriers that get in the way of planning, and
- high-level observations about the pitfalls of not planning, and the benefits of planning,
- I wish to conclude with a simple observation: **it is never too early to start planning your exit.**

Some of the hard issues that need to be addressed can take years to implement so give yourself a fighting chance of getting it right and begin the journey now. A lesson can be learnt from observing equity investors. They won't invest in a business unless and until their exit strategy is first negotiated and documented.

13. Conclusion

FINAL RULE	The more complex your personal or financial affairs, the more the likely you'll require professional advice. Only then can you be certain that your Will is done properly and your broader estate planning needs satisfied.

PROFESSIONAL INPUT OR DIY?

Estate Planning specialists guide you through a series of questions about your personal and financial affairs. They assess your individual requirements and provide advice. Often the first consultation is free and without obligation – check.

*Whether your needs are simple or complex, consulting an expert enables you to make an **informed decision** about what you wish to put into place, including the need for a business succession plan where appropriate.*

Newsagency Wills and other template products offer no assessment of your actual requirements, no individual advice and no education about the issues. You use them in a vacuum, remaining blissfully ignorant of issues that you may need to address. Anyone can fill out these documents and imagine they've prepared their Will or broader estate plan satisfactorily. Fact is, they assume (but don't know) whether it's suitable or not. If you are the type of person who would happily walk through a mine field while blindfolded when there is safe alternative route available, then these products are for you.

That's a big difference between getting advice and DIY. One that matters.

SCHEDULE I

A check list of succession planning issues for consideration and (as appropriate) discussion with family members, or your professional advisors.

I. Protecting family wealth from
- a beneficiary's marriage failing
- a beneficiary becoming bankrupt
- a beneficiary being sued
- a beneficiary's mental incapacity
- a beneficiary being a spendthrift
- a beneficiary being drug or gambling dependent
- the risk associated with a spouse remarrying
- a beneficiary being vulnerable for some other reason
- intestacy of beneficiaries

2. Minimising family disputes
- treat beneficiaries fairly/equally and, if not, how to minimise risk of successful challenge
- document your rationale for decisions
- communicate intentions to beneficiaries – avoid surprises, unless of course they're nice surprises
- clarify treatment of gifts made during their lifetime – are they to be treated as an advance on an inheritance or in addition to an inheritance
- provide more to younger beneficiaries so they don't have to pay for their education out of their inheritance (when older siblings had that advantage while you were alive)

- fair distribution of family heirlooms
- make special provision for family business
- make special provision for large assets
- address loans given to beneficiaries
- allow for capital gains tax
- avoid conflicts of interest for executors and attorney

3. Cater for the needs of a blended family
- provide for children from a prior marriage
- balance needs of partner with children and step children
- utilise a Family Law binding financial agreement
- keeping family assets within your bloodline
- communicate plans to extended family to avoid disputes
- use of mutual Wills agreements to preserve assets for children when a spouse passes, especially in blended family situations

4. Ensure dependants are cared for
- nominate appropriate guardians
- communicate wishes to guardians
- boost estate funding to meet needs of beneficiaries using life insurance

5. Reduce the chance of successful claims against estate
- anticipate and address likely claims
- execute the Will properly
- store the Will safely (you can't imagine how many Wills are lost)
- document justification, that is write out or otherwise document the reasons for your actions
- communicate with beneficiaries while you're alive about your Will
- get advice on likely claims

6. Protect vulnerable beneficiaries
- financial protection for the disabled
- appoint appropriate guardians for minors
- create disability trust during your lifetime or in your Will
- ongoing care for disabled adult beneficiaries
- boost size of estate to provide for beneficiaries using life insurance

7. Optimise financial outcomes for beneficiaries
- co-ordinate specialist tax, legal, investment and planning advice for executor
- administer estate in tax effective manner
- integrate estate administration with appropriate strategies for beneficiaries

8. Assist children and grandchildren with education and housing
- whilst you're alive
- in the event of your death
- in the event of your children predeceasing you

9. Support philanthropy
- support philanthropy tax effectively during your life
- support philanthropy via your estate
- create a legacy through charitable giving (e.g. a gift to the Red Cross)

10. Optimise benefit from future inheritance
- protect inheritance from claims against the deceased's estate
- protect inheritance from creditors
- protect inheritance from legal action
- minimise taxation on inheritance

II. Protect family business interests
- plan for business succession
- ensure business succession integrates with your estate planning
- protect against key-person risk

I2. Implement appropriate powers of attorney
- for financial matters
- for legal matters
- for lifestyle matters
- for health matters

I3. Develop aged care plan
- plan ahead for aged care accommodation
- execute an advanced health care directive specifying what medical treatment you wish to have or refuse to have

SCHEDULE 2

The three-stage process of *Succession Planning*

1. **Identification of personal assets** and those in your broader estate such as assets owned jointly, or owned by trusts or companies
2. **Identification of potential risks** including, for example, your early death or the possible divorce or bankruptcy of a beneficiary
3. **Design and implementation of a plan** that incorporates all your assets and considers flexibility to accommodate future changes, risk minimisation, tax minimisation and succession issues.

Each step is a multi-disciplinary exercise that usually will require the co-ordinated involvement of your financial planner, accountant and legal advisers.

SCHEDULE 3 – ESTATE PLANNING SELF ASSESSMENT

Please complete details that are applicable to you. A 'Yes' answer to any question indicates you require specialist advice before you complete a Will.

	PLEASE ANSWER THE FOLLOWING QUESTIONS	YES/ NO
	If you have a spouse or de facto	
1	Does your partner have a condition that affects, or with the passing of time could affect, his/her **mental capacity** (e.g. Alzheimer's disease)?	
2	Does your partner have **serious problems handling money**, to the point where you would not want him/her having direct access to the assets in your estate?	
3	Are you and your partner having serious **relationship problems**, to the point where you are concerned that you and he/she might separate?	
4	Are there any other reasons why you might want to **exclude your partner** from your Will or limit the gift you make to him/her from your estate?	
5	Are you responsible for the care and upbringing of **someone else's child** (i.e. a child who is not your natural or adopted child)?	
6	Have you had a **son or daughter die leaving behind a child** or children of his or her own (i.e. do you have a grandchild or grandchildren from a son or daughter who has since died)?	
	If you have a blended family	

7	Does your partner have any **children from another relationship** (i.e. children that are not your natural or adopted children)?	
8	Do you have any **children from another relationship** (i.e. children that are not your current spouse/partner's natural or adopted children)?	
	If children may benefit	
9	Do you have a **child with a disorder** for whom special arrangements are needed in your Will?	
10	Do you have a child who has **serious problems handling money** and who you would not want having direct access to the assets in your estate?	
11	Do you have a child who is married or in a committed domestic relationship and having serious **relationship problems** with his/her spouse/partner, to the point where you are concerned that they might separate?	
12	Do you have a child whom you want to **exclude from your Will** or give a much smaller share of your estate than your other children?	
	Other Issues	
13	Do you wish to make a **specific gift** to someone when you die, even if your spouse/partner survives you?	
14	Do you want to leave someone a **gift** in your Will that is **subject to** them satisfying a particular condition (other than them living longer than you and/or reaching a given age)?	
15	Do you want to leave someone a **'life interest'** (i.e. a gift of assets or a share of your estate which they enjoy while they are alive and which passes automatically to someone else when they die)?	

16	Do you want to leave a **gift of specific shares** in a company or other securities to someone in your Will?	
17	Do you want to leave a **gift of specific real estate** to someone in your Will?	
18	Do you want to make a **gift** to a beneficiary **subject to them taking over a debt** or mortgage (rather than that debt or mortgage being paid out by your estate, which is what would normally happen)?	
19	Do you or your spouse/partner control a **family company** or have shares in any private (non-listed) company that may need special consideration in your Will?	
20	Do you or your spouse/partner control a **family trust** or have units in any private (non-listed) unit trust that may need special consideration in your Will?	
21	Do you or your spouse/partner operate a business or have an interest as a partner in a **partnership** that may need special consideration in your Will?	
22	Do you or your spouse/partner own **substantial assets**, especially real estate, **outside Australia**?	
23	Are you or your spouse/partner subject to any **agreement or court order** that restricts your ability to transfer your assets or that could otherwise affect the distribution of your estate?	
24	**Discretionary testamentary trusts (see notes below)**	
	Do you want to include a discretionary testamentary trust in your Will?*	

* If
  - your estate is substantial; and/or
  - income producing assets will be left to beneficiaries; and/or
  - one or more beneficiary is at risk of divorce, bankruptcy, is a spendthrift, suffers a mental incapacity, or has a gambling, drug or alcohol dependency,
  - one or more beneficiary is under the influence of a person you are concerned about,

  then you should consider including a discretionary testamentary trust in your Will. In many circumstances substantial tax benefits and asset protection can be achieved by distributing assets to a trust rather than individual beneficiaries. The benefits, structure and type of trust vary with the circumstances.

ENDNOTES

1. The same applies for Enduring Power of Attorney, Appointment of Enduring Guardian and Advanced Health Care Directive – but more about those later.

2. I co-researched an article on DIT Will kits for *Choice Magazine*. See the article at: www.choice.com.au/money/financial-planning-and-investing/financial-planning/articles/will-kit-reviews.

3. The same can be said of the other essential documents: Enduring Power of Attorney, Appointment of Enduring Guardian and Advanced Health Care Directive.

4. Trustee Companies are commercial corporations or state-backed bodies that offer executor and estate administration services in completion with lawyers.

5. The figure of 33% is calculated by comparing 2016 ABS national marriage and divorce rates.

6. Section 106 Succession Act 2006 NSW.

7. Caution: this isn't an actual Will clause, just a lay version of what a clause aims to achieve.

8. I say 'notional share' because no beneficiary of a discretionary trust has any entitlement to income or property of the trust. You only get what the trustee decides to give you. If the trustee gives you nothing – that's all you'll get. With very rare exceptions (involving costly litigation), you'll have no remedy and have no access to trust property.

9. The survivor may lose capacity and their child (who holds the survivor's EPOA) could use their power to sell assets or otherwise deal with the survivor's assets to frustrate the terms of the survivor's Will and favour theirself.

10. At the time of authoring this book the NSW Law Reform Commission is reviewing the need and the options for legislation which grants executors greater access to digital assets.

11. Refer to the next heading for details about guardianship.

12. Sometimes called a living Will – refer to the next heading for more details.

13. Rates of tax applicable to 2013/14 tax year and subject to change.

14. Trust distributions to minors are taxed at 45%.

15. The calculations are based on the individual tax rates for the 2014/2015 tax year and are subject to change.

16. In a testamentary trust minors can receive tax free distributions up to $18,200 (2014/2015) or $20,542 (if low income tax offset applies).

17. Ian Raspin is a chartered accountant who specialises in the taxation of deceased estates and trusts. His firm is BNR Partners and his contact details are: Melbourne (03) 9781 6800 | Adelaide (08) 7221 9750 | Brisbane (07) 2101 5390 | Perth (08) 6323 5480 | Sydney (02) 9131 4270.

18. Caution: this and the next chapter are of a general nature only and not tailored to your specific circumstances. They may provide you guidance about the process but shouldn't be relied upon to make decisions. It is essential that you obtain your own individual advice from an expert.

19. Ian is a certified practicing accountant who specialises in the taxation of deceased estates and trusts. His firm is BNR Partners and his contact details are: Melbourne (03) 9781 6800 | Adelaide (08) 7221 9750 | Brisbane (07) 2101 5390 | Perth (08) 6323 5480 | Sydney (02) 9131 4270.